Eureka! to Market:

A GUIDE FOR ACADEMIC ENTREPRENEURS

Nicos Rossides

Published by Stoic Owl Press

First Edition

ISBN (Print Edition): 979-8-35093-034-4
ISBN (eBook Edition): 979-8-35093-035-1

AUTHOR BIOGRAPHY:

Dr. Nicos Rossides is a seasoned CEO, respected management consultant, and startup coach. His career spans multiple sectors, including academia and industry, where he has held leadership roles in global corporations, marketing insights agencies, and academic incubators. He is recognized for his expertise in combining academic rigor with managerial relevance and for setting up successful entrepreneurial ventures.

Dr. Rossides co-owns MASMI Research Group, a marketing insights agency with a wide network of offices across Central and Eastern Europe, as well as the Middle East. He also co-founded DMR, a digital marketing insights agency based in London, and currently serves as the Chairman of its Advisory Board.

As the CEO of CREF Business Ventures, an incubator associated with The Cyprus Institute, Dr. Rossides mentors and guides founders of academic spinoffs, assisting them in crafting and implementing effective go-to-market strategies.

Dr. Rossides has a long history in senior management roles. He honed his leadership skills at several global organizations, including Medochemie, an international pharmaceutical company, and Synovate, a top-four global marketing insights firm, where he served as CEO for EMEA & Global Solutions. His extended tenure as MEMRB International's CEO spanned nearly two decades before it was acquired by Aegis (Synovate's parent company).

He started his academic journey in the United States as a Fulbright scholar, earning both his Bachelor's and Master's degrees. He then attended Japan's prestigious Kyoto University, where he received his Doctor of Engineering degree and continued in postdoctoral and teaching capacities. After transitioning to his professional career, he engaged deeply in marketing insights, a career that spanned over 25 years. Before assuming his first international CEO role, he received his senior management training at MIT's Sloan School.

Dr. Rossides' most recent book, *Engaging the Workforce: The Grand Management Challenge of the 21st Century,* was published by Routledge/ Taylor & Francis in 2023. This work offers a unique perspective on the modern challenges of management. His other publications include *Exploring Japanese Culture: Not Inscrutable After All* (Matador, 2020), and a variety of insightful articles and white papers on management and innovation.

Dr. Rossides often speaks at international conferences and symposia. Additionally, he serves on the boards of several companies, including 6 academic startups.

ACKNOWLEDGMENTS:

I am deeply grateful to Fabio Montagnino, who not only penned the foreword to this book but also acted as an invaluable sounding board throughout its creation. His insights, critiques, and unwavering encouragement greatly enriched this work.

My heartfelt appreciation goes to Ryan Rutan, a cherished friend from our shared past and a luminary in today's startup world. Ryan's evolution, from our collaborative days to becoming a central figure in the global startup ecosystem with Startups.com and his enlightening Startup Therapy Podcast, speaks volumes about his dedication and expertise. His feedback, rooted in real-world experiences, offered a distinctive perspective that greatly influenced this book's content. Ryan's commitment to uplifting founders, coupled with his profound grasp of the startup milieu, has been invaluable.

I also wish to thank Dr. Marios Demetriades, now at the University of Cyprus; Professor Veljko Milutinovic of Purdue University and Indiana University; and Dr. Sarah Macnaughton, Britta Wyatt, and the stellar team at Oxford University's innovation consultancy, Oxentia. Their collective endeavors during the nascent stages of The Cyprus Institute's innovation ecosystem profoundly influenced our innovation approach. Our lively debates, occasional differences, and shared journeys provided invaluable insights into this complex yet captivating field. I am genuinely thankful for their contributions.

Lastly, to the founders and researchers I've had the honor of mentoring, your zeal, innovation, and drive have been truly inspiring. Our shared path, replete with both hurdles and successes, was an enlightening journey. Thank you for teaching me as much as I endeavored to impart to you.

CONTENTS

EUREKA! TO MARKET
BOOK ILLUSTRATIONS

1. Oxford University
2. Trivium & Quadrivium (2.1 and 2.2)
3. Bourdieu's Forms of Capital
4. C.P. Snow
5. Stanford University
6. Journal of Business Venturing
7. Gene Editing
8. Technology Readiness Levels
9. Google
10. Academia Vs Practice
11. Oxbotica
12. Triple Helix
13. Forms of IP
14. Genentech
15. The Valley of Death
16. The Four Phases of Startups
17. Product Market Fit
18. Oxford Nanopore
19. The Three Disciplines
20. The Business Model Canvas
21. GTM Strategy
22. Palantir
23. Slack

Eureka! to Market:

A GUIDE FOR ACADEMIC ENTREPRENEURS

FOREWORD BY
FABIO MONTAGNINO

Transitioning scientific research into a successful business venture demands courage, ingenuity, and foresight. It's a big leap from the world of academia to the business world—a leap fraught with immense challenges, yet one that could be incredibly rewarding. For scholars embracing the creation of deep tech start-ups, the process might seem surprisingly familiar—it is, in essence, another experiment. It involves posing questions, conducting trials, facing occasional failures, and making discoveries.

Success isn't guaranteed, but for those open-minded and newly-minted founders, this journey can illuminate the path from the lab to impactful innovation. As someone who has dedicated two decades to facilitating this transformation, I'm honored to contribute to this insightful guide, skillfully compiled by my esteemed colleague and friend, Nicos.

During our concerted efforts to cultivate an innovation ecosystem at The Cyprus Institute, our mission went beyond the traditional confines of evaluating academic research for commercial suitability. We sought to ignite a spark that would inspire the transformation of scholarly studies into impactful ventures. The founders we worked with were, by their nature, risk-takers, but they also harbored a powerful desire to make a meaningful difference—to see their work have an impact in the real world.

Our goal was not just to establish profitable businesses. We aimed higher: to revolutionize the mindset of academics, challenging them to see beyond theories and toward real-world applications that make a difference. We also wanted to foster a new paradigm in which industry and society at large could recognize the value and potential of academic innovations.

We sought to be catalysts, to set off a chain reaction of innovation and change. We didn't just want to transfer technology or commercialize ideas. We wanted

1

to create a culture of entrepreneurship inside academia, where people believe in the power of ideas to effect tangible change, disrupt existing systems, and create new possibilities.

Our ambition was to cultivate an environment that would empower academics to become pioneers, to leverage their intellectual rigor, curiosity, and creativity to forge new paths. We desired to create a setting where ideas could be nurtured, where innovation could thrive, and where novel solutions could be developed to address real-world challenges.

Our work was thus more than an innovation initiative; it was an endeavor to redefine the role and potential of academia in our society. It was about building a bridge between the academic world and the marketplace and demonstrating the extraordinary potential that can be realized when these two worlds converge.

Innovation & Entrepreneurship offices or Technology Transfer units serve as vital conduits between academia and industry in this transformation. Our initiatives include awareness campaigns featuring lectures, seminars, workshops, and engaging academics in diverse informal conversations. This is an ongoing task but particularly pertinent at the outset of building an ecosystem. Once ideas were hatched and vetted, we embarked on a systematic "translation" that may have included eventual venture creation. This often commenced with safeguarding intellectual property, creating a form of "dowry" for future entrepreneurs.

Our goal, however, was not to strike the most lucrative deal. Instead, we strived for fair agreements that would allow the technology to mature and make an impact. What is more, we approached each negotiation with a win-win mindset and intent.

Our team operated within clearly articulated, consistently enforced policies, even as the innovation ecosystem was evolving—a process akin to changing a car's tires while it's still in motion. Despite the constant challenge of minimizing bureaucracy, we managed to encourage creativity within a structured framework. We assembled a team with both technical acumen and business experience, enabling them to fluently speak both the language of academia and the business world. Their unwavering dedication to our mission and the burgeoning interest among students and faculty became the propelling force behind our innovation ambitions.

Our journey reaffirmed several crucial lessons. First, venture creation necessitates academics willing to step out of their comfort zones and strive for more than just producing publications. Second, simplicity is key—clear policies and unwavering leadership support pave the way for innovation—not ambiguity or ambivalence. Third, patience is paramount. Cultivating a thriving ecosystem requires time, acceptance of failures, policy adjustments, and alignment and motivation of different stakeholders. There are no ready-to-adopt models—transferred from elsewhere.

As you get immersed in this important book, I hope that Nicos' shared lessons will illuminate your path from academic innovation to entrepreneurial success. While the journey may be daunting, the potential to create a lasting impact is truly immense.

To those academic entrepreneurs embarking on this adventure, remember—you are the architects of our future society. As you bravely step forward, understand that you're not alone. With mentors like Nicos at your side, you're well-prepared for the challenging yet potentially thrilling expedition that lies ahead.

Fabio Montagnino
Governing Board—EIT Climate KIC Association
Former Director General of ARCA Consortium (Italy)
Director of Innovation & Entrepreneurship, The Cyprus Institute

CHAPTER 1:
Crossing Boundaries—
A Personal Journey

Throughout my career spanning over three decades, I had the opportunity to wear multiple hats—corporate CEO, entrepreneur, consultant, and startup coach. A key part of this journey was spent in corporate management, where critical discussions were shaping our organization's path forward. We grappled with strategic questions: Should we set up our own offices or expand through acquisitions? Is our organizational structure fit for purpose, or does it need a shake-up? How can we best engage and motivate our workforce while also attracting new talent, especially given shifting demographic trends? How can we adjust our strategies and operations to keep pace with fast-emerging technological advancements? And how do geopolitical changes affect our market positioning and strategy?

These conversations, primarily centered on growth and change, were guiding our organizational journey. They were infused with a sense of anticipation and excitement, even against a backdrop of uncertainties—the unsettling prospect of technological disruptions being a case in point. The decisions we made had far-reaching effects, touching everything from day-to-day operations to long-term strategic planning.

The growth-oriented mindset still prevails today, both in established corporations and, more overtly, in startups. In the context of new ventures, rapid growth is seen as the measure of success, especially during early-stage development. Yet, this growth imperative is increasingly scrutinized, given emerging societal awareness of finite environmental resources. This societal shift has prompted a reevaluation of the principles of perpetual growth. It nudges us towards alternatives that prioritize sustainability and viability not tethered to constant expansion.

This brings us to the heart of a paradox that startups face as they transition from early development to a more mature phase. At the start, new ventures need growth to succeed; it's an imperative. However, as they become viable, the growth model should be viewed through the lens of sustainable viability, not necessarily continual rapid growth. It's a delicate balancing act between the demands of the present and the requirements of a sustainable future.

The experience I gained during my immersion in corporate management was instrumental in shaping my career. It gave me a first-hand perspective on the hard choices organizations must confront and the strategies required to manage a successful company while balancing diverse stakeholder needs. I learned that the business context is always in flux, and adaptability is a defining characteristic of successful organizations. Above all, it became all too evident to me that resilience during tough times and agility in seizing opportunities distinguishes thriving organizations from those that struggle to keep pace.

A particularly transformative chapter in my journey was my tenure as CEO at MEMRB International, which coincided with a significant geopolitical shift—the fall of the Berlin Wall. Sensing an immense opportunity, we took decisive action to extend our reach into Central and Eastern Europe and the former Soviet Union. This strategic move, while laden with uncertainties and risks, promised the potential of new markets and access to a pool of highly educated researchers. It was a venture into unexplored territories that significantly altered our organization's scope and influence. It also made us an attractive proposition for potential acquirers—as it soon became apparent.

The fruits of our expansions weren't just about staking claims on new territories; it also involved cultivating high-performing companies within these new markets. This achievement drew the attention of Aegis, a global media buying and planning giant headquartered in London. They were in the process of developing a new marketing insights business, initially known as Aegis Research, later to be branded Synovate. Our successful growth aligned perfectly with their strategic blueprint, leading to our acquisition and incorporation into their evolving global network.

Under the leadership of global CEO Adrian Chedore, Synovate quickly matured and developed rapidly, posing a formidable challenge to industry titans such as Kantar, GfK, and Ipsos—growing both organically and through a series of highly targeted acquisitions.

However, the story came full circle when Synovate itself was acquired by IPSOS, an even larger global player which effectively ended the brand's remarkably successful growth journey. But I wouldn't trade the exhilarating experience for anything. During this time, I accumulated more air miles than I could conceivably exhaust in a lifetime and learned a valuable lesson about the Darwinian corporate world: it's a game of "eat or be eaten."

This period did more than just lay a solid foundation for my understanding of business dynamics and corporate decision-making. It emphasized the essence of strategic choices—the art of discerning not only what actions to pursue but also, crucially, recognizing what NOT to do. This discernment, I am convinced, is the quintessence of strategic thinking. And central to this approach is a salient truth: you can't be all things to all people; you must choose your battles and carefully define your territory.

Moreover, the experience instilled in me an understanding of the indispensable role of innovation in the creation and subsequent life cycle of companies. The ability to innovate and remain agile is an oft-repeated prescription for success, bordering on a cliché, but it is much more than just a slogan; it is truly the cornerstone of competitiveness, ensuring corporate viability.

My subsequent transition into the world of entrepreneurship and academic startups provided a fresh vista, even as certain themes and challenges remained constant. This new path held more than the exhilarating thrill of evaluating potentially groundbreaking scientific discoveries and seeing them through to become real-world solutions for our clients. It involved unveiling potential in the most unlikely places, challenging established paradigms, and daring to venture into uncharted territories.

The excitement of this journey wasn't drawn from just the intrigue of the unknown, but rather from the subtle, profound joy of discovery and progress—the opportunity to make a tangible difference. Whether it was in driving technology transfer or turning promising research into viable products, the persistent theme was innovation and its transformative power.

During this journey, interacting with founders—including my own experiences in this role—created a solid base of knowledge to draw from, continually enhancing and building on that foundation. Scholars turned founders, with their sometimes audacious vision and determination to invent and create impact, are the driving force of new ventures. Their willingness to question established norms and to venture into new exploration and testing is what inspired this book and, indeed, the journey of every academic startup.

During my current phase of coaching startups, I frequently tap into the insights and lessons from my earlier corporate tenure, especially from my involvement in over 20 strategic acquisitions. In that corporate phase, our focus was on acquiring smaller, innovation-driven enterprises with dynamic and nimble teams. Our ambitions stretched beyond merely marking our global footprint by adding more "dots on the map." We aimed to integrate these agile, creative units into our larger structures, boosting our expertise in crucial areas for decision support. Innovation became pivotal to our strategy to offer cutting-edge solutions for our clients—utilizing tools like brand equity measurement, ad tracking, market mix modeling, customer loyalty assessment and management, and product testing, among others.

This corporate chapter of growth and acquisitions provided a deep dive into the intricate link between innovation and the evolving business dynamics defining the intensely competitive global marketing insights arena. This is well aligned with Peter Drucker's idea that innovation serves as the vital pulse of organizations, marking their viability and longevity. Engaging with diverse teams, crafting myriad go-to-market (GTM) strategies, and steering acquisitions made me recognize the potent synergy of innovation and meticulous execution—an insight that continues to mold my viewpoints and strategies today.

Upon transitioning back into academia, particularly within the thriving innovation ecosystem, I felt a revived enthusiasm not just in producing new knowledge, but in leveraging this knowledge to conceive products and services meeting genuine customer needs. The focus shifted towards crafting knowledge with societal significance and impact, not restricted to purely commercial gains. Yet, a marked divide persists between the realm of scientific conjectures and their tangible application—a daunting divide that often proves too challenging to bridge.

Indeed, the success of any venture relies on more than just brilliant ideas. Running a successful business demands an understanding and navigation of a distinct realm—a world where the prevailing logic is steered by market traction, profitability, risk management, and stakeholder satisfaction. This realm stands in stark contrast to the theoretical frameworks and academic rigor of the university lab. The personas of a scholar and a business leader differ profoundly, transcending mere differences in style and demeanor. At their core, they embody different priorities, perspectives, and even philosophies.

This chasm tends to be further exacerbated by numerous challenges, such as insufficient business acumen, the lack of resources to commercialize research findings, the inherent risks accompanying the launch of new ventures, and the striking contrast in urgency between academic pursuits and business ventures. Making the leap from academia to business necessitates not just the acquisition of a new skill set, but also a significant paradigm shift—from intellectual curiosity and theory development to an unwavering emphasis on commercial viability and market impact.

Perceiving an opportunity to help bridge this gap, I assumed the role of an "academic entrepreneur" or "pracademic," dedicated to guiding academic startups on their journey towards value creation and capture. The transformation of nascent ideas born within the seclusion of university labs into market-ready solutions elicits a profound sense of accomplishment, especially since it is far from straightforward. Indeed, new ventures may fail due to various reasons—untimely market entry, lack of financial backing, or the brutal reality of surviving in highly competitive markets. And founders often overlook an important axiom for success—not only mastering the new language of business, but adapting to local contexts and cultures. Nonetheless, successful ventures are a testament to the fact that innovative ideas, pursued with tenacity and discipline, can indeed create significant market traction.

This book attempts to distill the essence of my diverse experiences into actionable insights, equipping you with the understanding needed to craft effective go-to-market (GTM) strategies. The upcoming chapters will explore the evolving role of research universities in fostering innovation, unravel the fundamental tenets of entrepreneurship, and examine critical concepts such as the valley of death and Technology Readiness Levels.

Designed as a comprehensive guide, this book provides a roadmap to help you navigate the key steps of your startup journey, including the pivotal stage of achieving a strong product-market fit. It draws attention to the distinctive challenges and opportunities academic startups encounter as they forge their paths in competitive markets. To illuminate the book's main themes, we examine real-world case studies, extracting critical lessons from both successful ventures and those that stumbled along the way.

It's easy to forget that many of our everyday products find their origins in university research labs. Often, the link between these products and their academic beginnings is obscured, as the innovation spotlight tends to focus on the private sector and the iconic companies that we so heavily rely on. Tech giants like Google and Microsoft have the capacity to swiftly turn groundbreaking ideas into market-ready solutions that most of us seek and use, so the limelight usually shines on them. Still, it's important to acknowledge that these corporations rely heavily on the fruits of rigorous academic research and the talents nurtured within university walls.

Real Innovation vs. Pseudo-Innovation

Through my career, I have come to appreciate the importance of genuine innovation. I have seen how it can improve the status quo, create new value for customers, and solve real problems. I have also witnessed the other end of the innovation spectrum, where change is introduced in ways that are cosmetic, more mirage than substance.

The key to success for any venture, whether it is based on genuine innovation or pseudo-innovation, is an intimate understanding of the target market. This means understanding the customer's needs, wants, and pain points. It also means understanding the competitive landscape and how the venture can differentiate itself from the competition.

Pseudo-innovations are products or services that are marketed as novel but closely mirror existing solutions without adding new value. They are essentially "me-too" offerings, echoing what is already in the marketplace, with only slight or cosmetic modifications. They may introduce features advertised as innovative, but they lack the transformative punch that true innovation brings. They typically compete on price and extensive marketing, which can put a squeeze on profit margins and are ultimately a weak business model.

Whether a venture leans on authentic innovation or finds itself in the domain of pseudo-innovation, the universal linchpin to success is an intimate understanding of the target market. This theme forms a cornerstone of our discussions, serving as a critical adjunct to crafting an effective go-to-market strategy.

The most groundbreaking innovations still need to harmonize with the idiosyncrasies of local markets, where elements like cultural sensitivities, regulatory frameworks, and consumer behaviors shape product receptivity. On the flip side, even offerings with modest novelty can carve out their niche if they adeptly cater to local preferences—be it convenience, cost, or a unique selling proposition—especially when they resonate with a particular audience segment.

As this introductory chapter comes to a close, I'd like to distill the purpose of this book: to provide you with straightforward tools and strategies to successfully navigate the valley of death and convert academic research into viable businesses. Think of this book as a compass and an ally, offering insights throughout your entrepreneurial journey. Whether you're an academic exploring the startup world or someone curious about the intersection of innovation, entrepreneurship, and the application of academic discoveries, this guide aims to light your way, sharing valuable insights, practical advice, and new perspectives on the journey from concept to market.

CHAPTER 2:

The Historical Evolution of Universities

The modern university is a product of a long and winding history. Its roots can be traced back to ancient institutions such as the Library of Alexandria in Egypt and the philosophical academies of Greece.

The Library of Alexandria was not a university in the modern sense, but it served as an intellectual hub for scholars from diverse fields. It played a significant role in the advancement of knowledge during antiquity and laid the foundation for academic exploration.

The philosophical academies of Socrates, Plato, and Aristotle pursued learning in the form of a dialogue between teacher and student. They nurtured intellectual development, not unlike how today's universities strive to do, effectively combining philosophical discourse with mentorship.

Aristotle's mentorship of Alexander the Great provides an often-cited example of the student-teacher relationship in ancient times. The philosopher guided the future conqueror's personal and intellectual growth before he embarked on his expeditions across the known world. This ancient model of instruction laid the groundwork for a more formalized educational institution, which, over centuries of evolution, developed into the modern university system.

The establishment of universities as formal institutions for advanced learning and scholarly research began to crystallize during the Middle Ages, specifically around the 11th and 12th centuries. The University of Bologna in Italy, founded in 1088, and the University of Paris, established around 1150, are often recognized among the world's oldest universities.

In the English-speaking world, the University of Oxford, established in the 12th century, bears the distinction of antiquity. Additionally, the University of Cambridge, founded in 1209, is another venerable institution that emerged during this period, contributing to a long lineage of historic centers of learning.

These early universities were founded by religious orders and were primarily focused on the study of theology. However, they also offered courses in law, medicine, and the liberal arts. Students from all over Europe came to these universities to study, and they quickly became centers of intellectual activity and debate.

The universities of the Middle Ages were centers of learning and culture. They attracted students from all over Europe and played a significant role in the development of Western civilization.

In the centuries that followed, universities continued to evolve. They became more secular and began to offer a wider range of courses. They also became more independent from the Church.

Early intellectual hubs weren't just driven by the quest for truth and the acquisition of knowledge. They were deeply engaged in ethical exploration, too, examining the moral and ethical dimensions of human existence. The Greek concept of *eudaimonia* translates to a "well-lived life" or a "fulfilling, virtuous life." Etymologically, *eudaimonia* is a fusion of *eu* (good) and *daimon* (spirit). At its core, it highlights the pursuit of personal excellence based on the recognition and realization of one's unique talents and potential.

Although these early academic assemblies differed in structure and scope from modern universities, they shared a vital, timeless objective: the quest for knowledge, truth, and wisdom, an aspiration that forms the bedrock of academic institutions, then and now.

The universities of the Middle Ages played a significant role in the development of Western civilization. They helped to spread knowledge and learning, and they trained the next generation of leaders and thinkers. They also helped to promote the development of new ideas and technologies.

(FIGURE 1: OXFORD UNIVERSITY)

These medieval universities primarily focused their education on the liberal arts, comprised of the *trivium* and the *quadrivium*.

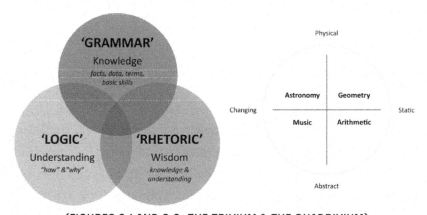

(FIGURES 2.1 AND 2.2: THE TRIVIUM & THE QUADRIVIUM)

The *trivium*, derived from the Latin word meaning "three ways," formed the foundation of a medieval liberal arts education. It consisted of grammar, logic, and rhetoric. Grammar, commonly associated with language study, served a broader purpose in the trivium, providing the foundational skills for reading and writing effectively. Logic, or dialectic, encouraged critical thinking and the art of asking meaningful questions to gain a better understanding of a subject. Finally, rhetoric, often misunderstood as mere persuasive language, represented the art of effective communication, with a strong emphasis on eloquence and persuasion.

Once students had a solid grasp of the trivium, they would advance to the *quadrivium*, comprising arithmetic, geometry, astronomy, and music. The *quadrivium*, originating from the Latin word for "four ways," focused on numerical and spatial relationships and understanding the universe's physical and metaphysical structures.

At this historical juncture, mastery of Latin and Greek was indispensable— serving as the *lingua franca* for academic discourse. If fact, these universities served as principal educational centers for clergymen and administrative officials, not just for those preparing to become teachers or professors.

In ancient India, the establishment of higher learning institutions like Takshashila and Nalanda University can be traced back to as early as the 6th century BCE and 5th century CE, respectively. These universities served as hubs for a wide array of subjects, from philosophy and astronomy to medicine and law, and played an important role in fostering intellectual curiosity and promoting societal enlightenment.

In China, the concept of higher learning is also deeply rooted. The Taixue, or "Great Learning", represented the pinnacle of education in China's early schooling system. Originating around the 2nd century BCE, during the Han Dynasty, the Taixue was more than an academic institution. It was a vital means for preparing students for civil service, tasked with nurturing intellectual elites who would play an important role in maintaining social order and a functioning bureaucracy. Thus, the Taixue can be seen as an early embodiment of the melding of academia and practical societal needs.

In Japan, the reverence for learning was equally embedded historically. The Ashikaga School was a distinguished center of learning during the Muromachi period, which stretched from the 14th to the 16th centuries. This period also witnessed the blossoming of the Keiō Gijuku University in the 19th century, an institution that played a key role in introducing and promoting Western learning during the transformative Meiji period. Since then, it has morphed into Keio University, one of Japan's well-known private universities.

In the subsequent stages of development, the emergence of Imperial Universities, notably Tokyo University and Kyoto University, significantly shaped Japanese academia and exerted considerable influence on society. Comparable to "Oxbridge" in the UK, these two universities have cultivated generations of intellectuals and political leaders, thus playing an outsized role in Japanese society. Their alumni often rise to influential positions in government and industry, which allows their alma maters to exert a disproportionate influence on the country's political, social, and economic life. The Imperial Universities, both then and now, showcase the profound symbiosis between academia and societal power structures, playing a crucial societal role in the process.

Universities, both Eastern and Western, have traditionally engaged in dual roles: the generation of knowledge and the shaping of society. Despite the varying geographical and cultural contexts, they have committed themselves to the nurturing, preservation, and spread of knowledge.

However, the application of this knowledge within society has significantly varied. In the Western tradition, higher education institutions became more than intellectual hubs; they were also the training ground for various professions, including clergy and lawyers. Consequently, their education extended beyond theoretical pursuits, ensuring graduates were well-equipped to practically contribute to society.

Conversely, Eastern institutions often emphasized preparing students for civil service roles, while also fostering intellectual growth. This focus helped to maintain societal order and nurture an educated elite class, albeit with a different scope and emphasis than their Western counterparts.

Pierre Bourdieu's theoretical framework provides a valuable lens for understanding the role of universities in society. His work centers on cultural capital and social reproduction, suggesting that higher education not only serves as a pathway for knowledge acquisition but also as a tool for maintaining societal hierarchies. Universities, in his view, are key to creating, distributing, and validating forms of cultural capital (Bourdieu, 1986).

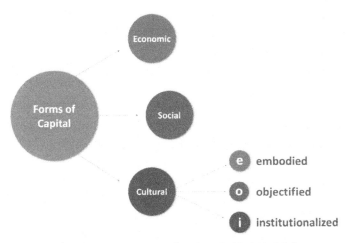

(FIGURE 3: BOURDIEU'S FORMS OF CAPITAL)

Bourdieu's cultural capital exists in three forms: embodied, objectified, and institutionalized. Embodied cultural capital refers to an individual's knowledge, skills, and education—all of which higher education enhances. Objectified cultural capital comprises cultural goods (books, art, scientific instruments) requiring cultural competencies for appreciation. Lastly, institutionalized cultural capital includes academic qualifications, such as degrees, that the labor market recognizes and rewards.

Higher education access grants these "learned elites" an advantage in accumulating cultural capital, thereby perpetuating their societal power status. By imparting this form of capital, universities consequently reinforce these elites' dominant position, affirming their own influence.

The evolution of universities reflects a myriad of societal norms and needs. From their inception, these institutions have been more than mere repositories of knowledge; they have been pillars of societal stability and growth, shaping policy decisions and societal norms.

The transition from the traditional university model to a research-based model marked a significant shift, particularly during the Post-WWII university expansion, largely due to the GI Bill. This period saw an increase in curriculum offerings, including creative fields such as literature and arts. This created a broader academic spectrum and fostered the emergence of a "cult of creativity," as noted by my long-time friend, literature professor, and eminent intellectual, Dr. Jan Gordon.

I discussed with him, at length, the evolving role of universities, especially the enduring value of the humanities. Indeed, he strongly holds the view that the humanities, though seldom producing traditional intellectual property, play a vital yet less direct role in societal advancement and innovation. He argues that the humanities, in shedding light on the human condition and expanding our collective consciousness, facilitate progress and change in a way that may be more nuanced and indirect, yet is indisputably influential and profound.

As societal priorities and expectations have shifted, so too has the focus of education. There has been a natural tilt towards disciplines with clear job market outcomes—a "utilitarian" emphasis reflecting the escalating costs of education and the growing demand for a direct return on this investment. This has inevitably led to the prominence of science, technology, engineering, and mathematics (STEM) fields, further fueled by increased demand in the job market for professionals with these skills and qualifications.

While this change has been driven by tangible economic and societal pressures, it is essential to recognize that education's role is not solely to meet immediate market needs. The value of an education system lies in its ability to foster intellectual growth, ethical reasoning, and an understanding of the complexities of the human condition—which is what the humanities bring to the table. Subjects like literature, philosophy, history, and social sciences bring a nuanced and expanded understanding of human behavior, cultural contexts, ethics, and critical thinking.

Of course, the shift in priorities has not been without complications. University research has increasingly drifted towards more practical applications—medical, defense-related, and other areas with direct societal or economic impact. Driven in part by the need for grant funding, this drift has created a contentious environment where the humanities and sciences often find themselves in stark opposition, with the latter being seen as the more societally relevant.

This tension is a modern reflection of the dichotomy articulated by C.P. Snow in his lecture "The Two Cultures," a depiction that still resonates today.

(FIGURE 4: C.P. SNOW)

Indeed, the humanities perspective remains pivotal in a world marked by sweeping technological advancements and societal shifts. When the focus on immediate job market applicability overshadows the nurturing of these insights, we risk impoverishing the overall quality of education. This may result in a generation of graduates who are technically skilled but lack the broader perspectives and critical thinking skills that the humanities cultivate.

The ramifications of this dichotomy are especially pronounced in fields where technology and human behavior intersect, such as User Experience (UX) Design. Here, the merits of a balanced, interdisciplinary approach become apparent, demonstrating the importance of uniting the strengths of both the humanities and the sciences.

In the mid-90s, Don Norman's seminal work at Apple triggered a paradigm shift towards a more human-centric approach in technology design. This reshaping of design philosophy underscores the inestimable value of humanities in creating intuitive, user-friendly, and engaging technological solutions—striving to bridge Snow's divide by fostering an interdisciplinary mindset and weaving various disciplines into their curricula. This shift is by no means easy; it involves juggling a set of expectations that are sometimes antithetical—to maintain the integrity of individual disciplines while encouraging a synthesis of knowledge.

Take, for example, the Massachusetts Institute of Technology (MIT) Center for Art, Science & Technology (CAST), which has pioneered innovative cross-disciplinary initiatives. These initiatives stimulate the convergence of disparate fields, fostering dialogues and collaborations between scientists, engineers, and artists. The ultimate aim is to cultivate an academic culture where exploration and innovation at the intersection of diverse disciplines are celebrated.

The AI Revolution in Learning & Research

As we venture deeper into the world of academic entrepreneurship, we must bear in mind the complex history and inherent tensions within universities. While grappling with this challenge, we should never lose sight of the collective contribution that all academic disciplines bring to societal progress, especially in light of the huge advances we see in digital and AI-powered capabilities.

One of the most significant impacts of AI and technology is on the way we learn. AI-powered learning platforms are becoming increasingly sophisticated and are able to provide personalized learning experiences. These platforms can track students' progress, identify areas where they need help, and provide tailored instruction. As a result, students are able to learn more effectively and efficiently.

AI is also having a major impact on research. AI-powered tools are being used to analyze large datasets, identify patterns, and make predictions. This is revolutionizing the way we conduct research and is leading to new discoveries in a wide range of fields.

Finally, AI is changing the way we interact with universities. Students are now able to access courses and resources online from anywhere in the world. This is making it possible for more people to get a university education, regardless of their location or circumstances.

The impact of AI and technology on the future of universities and startups is still unfolding and will be examined in more detail in the Chapters that follow. What is clear is that these technologies are having a profound impact on the way we learn, the way we research, and the way we launch and grow startups.

Here are some specific examples of how AI and technology are changing the future of universities and startups:

- Online learning: AI-powered learning platforms are making it possible for students to take courses online regardless of their location or circumstances. This online capability also makes it easier for startups to recruit talent from a global pool of candidates.

- Virtual reality (VR) and augmented reality (AR): VR and AR are being used to create immersive learning experiences. This can be used to simulate real-world experiences, such as conducting a medical procedure or performing a scientific experiment. This can be helpful for startups that are developing new products or services that require specialized knowledge or skills.

- Chatbots: Chatbots are being used to provide academic support to students. Chatbots can answer questions, provide feedback, and even help students with their coursework. This can free up time for professors and TAs to focus on more complex tasks, such as mentoring students and providing research support.

- Machine learning: Machine learning is being used to personalize learning experiences for students. Machine learning algorithms can track students' progress and use that information to identify areas where they need help.

These are just a few examples of how AI and technology are revolutionizing the way we learn, the way we research, and the way we launch and grow startups. And much more is sure to come in the years ahead.

The Rise of the Technology Transfer Office (TTO)

As universities continue to evolve in the digital age, they are increasingly turning to technology transfer offices (TTOs) to help them commercialize their research and create startups. Although formal TTOs have been around for decades, their significance is growing and their toolkits are becoming more varied, especially with developments in AI.

In the past, TTOs were primarily responsible for patenting and licensing university research. However, with the advent of new technologies, TTOs are now playing a more active role in helping startups to commercialize university research. For example, TTOs are now using AI-powered tools to identify potential startups that could benefit from university research. They are also providing startups with access to university resources, such as labs and equipment.

Additionally, TTOs are assisting startups in navigating the regulatory landscape and secure funding. Organized as dedicated Units or Departments, and drawing on internal as well as external resources, they face a number of challenges, such as the need to identify promising research projects, the cost of patenting and licensing, and the difficulty of commercializing university research.

As we further explore the commercialization world, it's crucial to highlight the evolving mandate of TTOs and how they may leverage technological advancements to enhance their effectiveness. They do more than just shepherd innovations to the market; they confer a wealth of expertise benefiting everyone—from the inquisitive academic and vested university to the zealous investor and the anticipatory public.

With this foundation laid, let's explore our first case study—a look into Stanford University's dynamic "lab to business venture" ecosystem.

CASE STUDY: STANFORD UNIVERSITY

Stanford University, founded in 1885 by Leland and Jane Stanford, initially adhered to the traditional European education model. But the arrival of Frederick Terman, frequently hailed as the "Father of Silicon Valley," ignited a transformative shift towards fostering innovation and entrepreneurship. This transformation became virtually synonymous with the university's image, *a beacon of innovation and entrepreneurship.*

(FIGURE 5: STANFORD UNIVERSITY)

Terman served as Stanford's provost during the 1950s and 1960s, and he played a key role in the university's transformation into an entrepreneurial hub. He believed that universities should play a more active role in commercializing research and fostering innovation. He also held the view that universities should create an environment that encourages students and faculty to start their own companies.

Today, Stanford University's idyllic campus in Silicon Valley belies its position as a global innovation powerhouse. Since the 1950s, the University has actively cultivated one of the world's most vibrant academic entrepreneurial ecosystems. This has led to the creation of thousands of companies spanning industries from technology to biotechnology.

Some prominent examples of influential companies founded by Stanford alumni include:

- Google - Co-founded by PhD students Larry Page and Sergey Brin in 1998, the tech giant evolved from an academic research project into the world's most popular search engine and a $1.6 trillion business.

- Cisco Systems - Founded in 1984 by a computer scientist couple, Leonard Bosack and Sandy Lerner, who pioneered multi-protocol router technology while working at Stanford. Cisco has become a worldwide leader in IT and networking.

- Netflix - Launched in 1997 by Stanford alum Reed Hastings after he was inspired to start a DVD rental by mail business. The company has disrupted entertainment and media, now valued at over $100 billion.

- LinkedIn - Created by Stanford students Reid Hoffman, Allen Blue, Konstantin Guericke, Eric Ly, and Jean-Luc Vaillant in 2002. The professional networking platform was acquired by Microsoft for $26 billion in 2016.

- Snapchat - Born out of a Stanford class project by Bobby Murphy and Evan Spiegel in 2011. The ephemeral photo messaging app now reaches over 300 million daily users.

In total, Stanford alumni have created over 70,000 companies since the 1930s, raising over $3 trillion in funding and generating revenues of $2.7 trillion annually. In 2020 alone, Stanford was granted 307 patents and helped launch 36 startups which raised a combined $5.4 billion in funding.

Behind these remarkable statistics is Stanford's multidimensional approach to entrepreneurship.

It maintains close industry ties through diverse initiatives such as:

- Research partnerships with corporations to develop commercially relevant technologies.

- Talent development programs like the Stanford Ignite certificate for budding entrepreneurs.

- On-campus incubators like StartX which has supported over 3,400 startups since 2009.

- Licensing innovations from Stanford research to external companies via its Office of Technology Licensing.

Through this robust entrepreneurial ecosystem orchestrated by forward-thinking university leadership, Stanford has solidified its reputation as a launchpad for world-changing innovation across industries. Its unique model has been mimicked by universities globally hoping to replicate its game-changing impact.

As we'll argue throughout this book, there is a lot that universities can do to help to foster the next generation of entrepreneurs and innovators. And Stanford is a great example to learn from.

CHAPTER 3:
Defining Innovation and Entrepreneurship

In an age of technological breakthroughs, dynamic markets, and a constant push towards the "next big thing," two concepts have emerged as the central driving forces behind modern economic growth and societal progress: innovation and entrepreneurship. Together, they form the lifeblood of our global economy, shaping industries, transforming communities, and influencing the very way we live, work, and think.

While closely interlinked, innovation and entrepreneurship have distinct characteristics that give them unique identities. Innovation is the creative spark that generates new ideas, technologies, or processes. Entrepreneurship is the engine that propels those innovations to market, converting ideas into profitable business ventures.

Though distinct, innovation and entrepreneurship share a profound symbiotic relationship. True innovation struggles to deliver impact in isolation, while entrepreneurship cannot thrive without a steady flow of innovations to propel new opportunities.

In contemporary academia these topics are taught at prestigious institutions worldwide, such as Harvard Business School, Stanford Graduate School of Business, and MIT's Sloan School of Management. Professors leading these courses often have a foot in both the academic and entrepreneurial worlds, evidence of the real-world significance and applicability of their expertise. They are trailblazers who turn eureka moments into valuable products and services that make a difference in the world.

The exploration of innovation and entrepreneurship has grown to become a field of study in its own right. Universities, think tanks, and corporate innovation labs worldwide explore the complex interplay between these forces, seeking to understand, harness, and cultivate them.

In this chapter, we will examine these complex concepts from multiple perspectives, including their etymology, the thoughts of seminal thinkers, and how they are both distinct and intertwined. It is a journey into the very heart of what makes our world tick.

This is not an academic exercise; it is a lens through which we can understand the mechanisms that drive change—a constant in our modern world. Whether you are a budding entrepreneur, an established business leader, or an intrigued observer, understanding innovation and entrepreneurship offers a roadmap to navigate the complex landscape of contemporary business and society.

Let us begin by first exploring the multifaceted concept of innovation.

Innovation: Sparks That Transform Our World

As I have argued earlier, genuine innovation is a new and novel approach that creates value. It is about solving real problems in new and creative ways, rather than making cosmetic changes that only change the appearance of a product or service without actually improving it. It is quintessentially about substance rather than optics.

The word "innovation" comes from the Latin word *innovatio*, meaning "renewal" or "change." It's a term that evokes a sense of transformation, a shift from the old to the new. Imagine a world where the wheel has never been invented. Life is laborious, transporting anything is a struggle, and progress is slow. Then, someone conceives the idea of the wheel. It's a simple idea, yet it changes everything. That's what innovation is about, and it is a uniquely human capability.

Although many scholars and practitioners view innovation and entrepreneurship as distinct yet closely intertwined concepts (a perspective I share), Joseph Schumpeter, an influential theorist in the early 20th century, saw them as virtually synonymous (Schumpeter, 1943). He famously coined the term "creative destruction" to describe the process of innovation as a fundamental causative factor behind change in capitalist society—one that needed entrepreneurs to become reality.

But Schumpeter's analysis extended beyond simply identifying innovation as a force of transformation; he also underscored its role in economic development's cyclical and evolutionary nature. For him, "carrying out innovations is the only function which is fundamental in history." What is more, he envisaged entrepreneurship as the engine that replaces "today's Pareto optimum with tomorrow's different new thing." Thus, in Schumpeter's view, entrepreneurship and innovation weren't merely interlinked; they were essentially synonymous.

Schumpeter's insights still shape how economists and business leaders think about change and progress today, challenging the view that entrepreneurship is a static achievement. Instead, it is a dynamic process, always moving toward new horizons and reshaping markets—a perspective that elevates the importance of continual innovation, adaptability, and the willingness to disrupt even successful models in the pursuit of long-term transformation and progress.

My own view is that the two have distinct essences, even as they share a profound symbiosis. True innovation struggles to deliver impact without entrepreneurial skill to bring it to market. And entrepreneurship falters without a steady influx of innovations to drive new opportunities.

So, entrepreneurship is more about execution, not just creativity. It is focused on turning ideas into enterprises that deliver value in the real world. Indeed, I argue throughout this book that understanding this dynamic interplay provides powerful insights into the engines that drive progress, growth, and lasting change.

Peter Drucker, another Austrian-born scholar and the father of modern management, argued that innovation is not solely a mystical talent but a discipline that can be learned and practiced (Drucker, 1985). To Drucker, innovation resembled learning a musical instrument, something anyone can master with practice, persistence, and creativity.

His insights demonstrated an ability to distill profound yet practical wisdom around the key notions of innovation and entrepreneurship and their relevance to societal development. Indeed, Drucker believed that entrepreneurship is the engine that drives innovation and that it is, therefore, a vital driving force for economic growth and development. By aligning innovation with an organization's strategic goals and understanding market needs, Drucker believed that businesses could make innovation both repeatable and sustainable through the endeavors of entrepreneurs.

Clayton Christensen, a more recent seminal thinker (1995), introduced the concept of "disruptive innovation" to explain how new ideas can reshape industries and markets. He saw it as a process where a product or service takes root in simple applications at the market's fringe and then moves upmarket, eventually displacing established competitors. He noted that companies often innovate faster than their customers' needs evolve, leading to products that are overly sophisticated, expensive, and complex. While these "sustaining innovations" may cater to high-end customers, they may also create opportunities at the market's lower end—which is where disruptive innovations find their footing.

A case in point is Netflix. Originally, it started as a mail-order DVD rental service, appealing to a niche market of movie enthusiasts. Over time, the company evolved into an online streaming platform, providing on-demand entertainment. It wasn't as high definition as cable TV initially, but it was good enough for customers looking for affordable and convenient options. As the company improved its service and content, it started to attract mainstream consumers, disrupting the established cable and satellite television industries.

Indeed, disruptive innovations tend to begin modestly, satisfying the needs of less-demanding customers. Over time, as they evolve and improve, they challenge and can even replace established industry players. This insight underscores that true innovation isn't merely about developing superior products for existing customers. It involves recognizing overlooked opportunities and daring to meet neglected needs.

Innovation, then, is not confined to grand ideas or inventions—those key *eureka* moments. It encompasses strategic insight, and understanding where and how to innovate. It manifests in daily life, from adapting recipes to personal taste, finding shortcuts on commutes, to rearranging desks for efficiency. At its core, innovation reflects an innate human desire to improve, to forge new paths, and to enhance life.

Entrepreneurship: An Attempt to Build Something New

At its core, entrepreneurship is the process of initiating, organizing, and managing a new venture. It is a risky undertaking that requires creativity, innovation, and a willingness to take risks. The term "entrepreneurship" is derived from the French verb *entreprendre*, which means "to undertake."

Other languages have terms with nearly identical connotations. In German, the word for entrepreneurship is *unternehmertum*, which is made up of the words *unternehmen* (company or enterprise) and *unternehmer* (entrepreneur).

In Greek, the closest terms are επιχειρείν (*epihirein*) which denotes an attempt to try something and επιχειρηματικότητα (from the root επιχείρηση, enterprise) which connotes the act of doing business.

Entrepreneurship has been a key human trait for centuries, but it is only recently that academia has begun to study it as a discipline. This has led to a surge of research on the topic, which has helped us to better understand the principles, dynamics, and potential of entrepreneurship.

Academic journals such as the *Journal of Business Venturing*, *Entrepreneurship Theory and Practice* and the *Strategic Entrepreneurship Journal* have published research on a wide range of topics related to entrepreneurship, including the determinants of entrepreneurial success; the role of personality and motivation in entrepreneurship; the impact of entrepreneurship on economic growth; and the challenges and opportunities facing entrepreneurs.

(FIGURE 6: JOURNAL OF BUSINESS VENTURING)

The plethora of articles and books has helped us to better understand the nature of entrepreneurship and the factors that contribute to its success. It has also helped to develop new theories and models of entrepreneurship that can be used to guide future research and practice, with a range of insights that now form the bedrock of our current understanding. As a complex process of creating new businesses and organizations, it is influenced by a variety of factors, including individual characteristics, environmental conditions, and economic opportunities.

There is no single formula for entrepreneurial success, but some of the key factors that contribute to success include:

- Creativity: come up with new ideas and solutions to problems.
- Innovation: bring new ideas to market and make them successful.
- Risk-taking: a willingness to take risks in order to achieve goals.
- Perseverance: persevere in the face of challenges.

And beyond its utility to the individuals involved, entrepreneurship can have a significant impact on economic growth by creating jobs, stimulating innovation, and driving competition. What is more, entrepreneurs also play a role in solving social problems by creating new products and services that meet the evolving needs of society.

So, the entrepreneur shifts the focus of the traditional managerial paradigm from control and efficiency to creativity and innovation—breaking free from old molds of what worked well. Management in this context becomes more about facilitation, enablement, creativity, and innovation. It becomes, quintessentially, an effort to create an environment where one feels safe to take risks and experiment.

The research on entrepreneurship is still in its early stages, but it has already made significant progress in helping us to understand its multiple facets and dynamics, at multiple levels. As research continues, we can expect to learn even more about the nature of entrepreneurship and how it can be promoted and supported.

Yet, the essence of entrepreneurship goes beyond the theories penned in journals and books on the subject. As Steve Blank (2013) emphasizes, true entrepreneurship is not just about ideas; it is quintessentially about action, trying different things, probing, and experimentation. Moving from the safe confines of labs to the unpredictable terrain of the real market, entrepreneurs face a direct confrontation with genuine needs and are constantly attuning to the ever-evolving market dynamics. But to me, the emphasis on real-world testing is not merely about the iterative nature of venture creation; it is also about revealing the deeper, personal motivations that fuel these efforts.

Entrepreneurs find themselves in a world where they must continuously adapt to new languages: the languages of customers, investors, and market trends. Yet, beneath these external dialogues, there is a personal narrative. Entrepreneurs are not solely motivated by profit or opportunity; they are often driven by passion, vision, and the burning desire to leave an indelible mark. To leave a legacy.

Indeed, the entrepreneurial journey involves a blend between external market realities and our emotions. Entrepreneurs must continually pivot their ventures in response to market signals while navigating their own ever-shifting mix of aspirations, hopes, fears, and doubts.

Entrepreneurship demands navigating a landscape of contrasts and contradictions. Alain Ehrenberg depicts the modern entrepreneurial self as constantly oscillating between ambitious aspirations and inherent challenges/fears (Ehrenberg, 2020). Taking inspiration from Roman mythology, I liken the entrepreneurial self to Janus, the two-faced god overseeing beginnings, transitions, and endings. One face projects resilience, vision, and determination. But its counterpart reveals vulnerabilities—the specters of stress, self-doubt, and potential failure.

This duality also resonates with Erich Fromm's "pathology of normalcy" (Fromm, 1963). He aptly observed that societal norms can distort certain traits deemed "normal," making them pathological. Individualism and selfishness are often seen as normal and even favorable personality traits, but in excess they can be very harmful. Likewise, celebrating entrepreneurs' strengths may neglect their fragility.

Understanding entrepreneurship requires recognizing this Janus-faced duality, a continuous balancing act between innovation's external demands and the internal push of apprehension. Embracing both the highs and lows allows more holistic, empathetic support for entrepreneurs.

Entrepreneurship, at its core, demands a balance of introspection and ambition. Beyond the risks and innovations, it's a deeply personal journey. It calls upon those who are not only willing to challenge the external world of markets and opportunities (represented by innovation) but also ready to grapple with their internal landscapes of fears, hopes, and dreams (the essence of entrepreneurship). It's a path that beckons the curious, the passionate, and those willing to delve deep into both the world around them and the world within.

Of course, the interplay between innovation and entrepreneurship can be complex, with many layers. Academic theories can help us explore and understand these layers. As the boundaries between theoretical insights and their practical applications become more porous, there arises a need to bridge the divide. How can we ensure that academic rigor not only remains relevant but actively contributes to our understanding of how enterprise and innovation co-exist and intetwine in the real world?

Professor Julian Birkinshaw of the London Business School (2012) champions an "ambidextrous" academic approach, one that aims to balance theoretical inquiry with dynamic practical application. By doing so, Birkinshaw posits that academia can effectively function as both a think-tank, generating rigorous models and theories, as well as a catalyst, driving real-world implementation.

The ensuing chapter delves into academic startups, highlighting their pivotal role in societal progress. They stand at the intersection of innovation and entrepreneurial spirit, converting academic insights into products and services. Before we journey further, the case of CRISPR Therapeutics will showcase the interplay between innovation and entrepreneurship and their collective transformative potential.

CASE STUDY: CRISPR THERAPEUTICS

Founded in 2013 by Nobel laureates Jennifer Doudna and Emmanuelle Charpentier, CRISPR Therapeutics stands at the forefront of the gene-editing revolution. Originating from groundbreaking research at the University of California, Berkeley, and the Broad Institute, the company is pioneering therapies using CRISPR technology to combat a spectrum of diseases, including cancer, blood disorders, and infectious diseases.

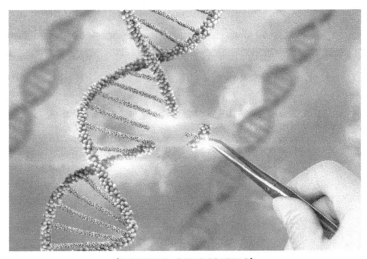

(FIGURE 7: GENE EDITING)

The company's innovation stems from leveraging a bacterial defense mechanism, transforming it into a precision tool capable of modifying specific DNA segments. This innovation, known as CRISPR-Cas9 technology, has set unprecedented standards in genetics and biotechnology, enabling precise alterations to DNA sequences and offering the potential to correct genetic defects and combat previously incurable diseases.

CRISPR-Cas9 allows for meticulous modifications to DNA, utilizing a protein, Cas9, to cut DNA at designated locations, enabling scientists to insert, delete, or replace specific DNA sequences. This revolutionary technology holds the promise of transforming medicine by developing novel treatments for a myriad of diseases.

CRISPR Therapeutics' Pipeline

CRISPR Therapeutics has developed a robust pipeline of innovative therapies, including:

- **CTX001**: The first FDA-approved CRISPR-based therapy for sickle cell disease and beta thalassemia in 2021.
- **CTX110**: Undergoing Phase 1 clinical trials, this therapy targets multiple myeloma.
- **CTX120**: A therapy for transfusion-dependent beta thalassemia, currently in Phase 1/2 clinical trials.
- **CTX130**: In Phase 1 clinical trials, targeting T-cell lymphoma.

The company has also forged partnerships with pharmaceutical leaders like Bayer, Vertex Pharmaceuticals, and ViaCyte to expand the development of CRISPR-based therapies.

Challenges and Future Directions

While CRISPR technology heralds a new era in medicine, it faces challenges, including potential off-target effects and the development of efficient and safe delivery methods for therapies. But the company remains steadfast in its commitment to overcoming these hurdles, aiming to revolutionize medicine through its CRISPR-based therapies.

Highlight: CRISPR Therapeutics exemplifies the transformative power of combining innovation with entrepreneurship, highlighting the significant role academic startups play in advancing industries and delivering societal benefits. The company's journey is a great example in the life sciences sector, showcasing the potential of CRISPR-Cas9 to redefine our approach to disease management and healthcare.

CHAPTER 4:
The Emergence of Academic Startups

Academic startups have carved a niche for themselves as a significant driver of economic development, a narrative shaped during the latter half of the 20th century. This was catalyzed by a confluence of societal, economic, and policy factors, notably the Bayh-Dole Act in the United States (enacted into law in 1980), which sparked academic entrepreneurship by allowing universities to retain intellectual property rights from federally funded research.

The emergence of academic startups was further bolstered by the establishment of a structured assessment framework known as Technology Readiness Levels (TRLs). This provides a systematic measure for evaluating the maturity of a particular technology and its readiness for market launch and commercial viability. Originally conceived by NASA in the 1970s, TRLs have served as an important tool for evaluating and bridging the gap between academic research and market-ready solutions.

The TRL scale spans from 1 (representing fundamental principles observed and reported) to 9 (indicative of an actual technology proven successful in an operational setting). This step-by-step progression offers a straightforward way to assess a technology's market readiness, from its earliest conceptualization in the laboratory to full deployment and operation in the real world.

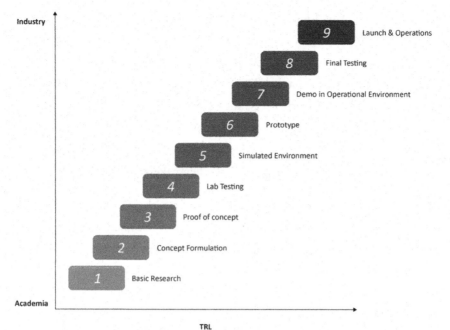

(FIGURE 8: TECHNOLOGY READINESS LEVELS)

Successful examples abound, even as many more have failed, languishing in obscurity, perhaps for obvious reasons. Who does not know:

- *23andMe*: This company developed a technology that allows people to learn about their ancestry and genetic makeup. The company started with a TRL of 1 and has now raised over $1 billion in funding. It is now a publicly traded company.

- Dropbox: This company developed a cloud storage service that allows people to store files online. The company started with a TRL of 2 and currently has over 700 million users. It is now a unicorn company, with a valuation of over $10 billion.

- *Airbnb*: This company developed a platform that allows people to rent out their homes to travelers. Airbnb started with a TRL of 3 and now has over 4 million listings in over 190 countries. It is a publicly-traded company.

Over the years, the TRL framework has gained recognition beyond its origins at NASA and has been adopted by various international organizations. Notably, the European Union's Horizon 2020 program and the U.S. Department of Defense have utilized TRLs to classify the maturity of technologies involved in their projects. Such a structured, objective, and globally recognized system significantly simplifies discussions on technological progress. It offers a common language for a wide range of stakeholders, be they researchers, entrepreneurs, investors, or policymakers.

Typically, academic startups begin their journey with a technology that falls between levels 1 and 3 on the TRL scale. Early on, their main challenge lies in moving their technology up the ladder towards market readiness. This is often achieved while navigating the valley of death—a phase in the startup journey that marks the demise of promising ideas. This may be due to insufficient resources (notably cash) and a critical lack of commercial traction.

The Evolution of Academic Entrepreneurship

The emergence of academic startups didn't occur overnight but reflected an evolution in the role of universities and their relationship with industry. In the early 20th century, academic culture generally emphasized pure scientific research and education over commercial applications. However, pioneering universities like MIT and Stanford began forging connections with industry.

For instance, in 1912, MIT established the country's first university-based industrial research laboratory sponsored by General Electric. This represented an early university-industry alliance focused on applied research.

Similarly, in the 1920s and 30s, Stanford's Dean of Engineering Frederick Terman spearheaded collaborations between Stanford and technology firms like Hewlett-Packard, shaping the genesis of Silicon Valley.

Such partnerships dispelled notions that academia should shy away from research with commercial potential. They laid the foundations for a more actively engaged model of universities focused on commercializing discoveries, which accelerated after World War 2, especially after the passing of the Bayh-Dole Act in the US.

In the decades since, many nations have enacted similar legislation, like Japan's TLO Act of 1998, which similarly spurred growth in academic startups. Germany's Employee Invention Act of 2002 had a comparable impact. In addition to setting up institutional frameworks, governments also played a key role in fostering innovation and economic growth by providing targeted support to key industries. For example, the Finnish government's support of Nokia in the 90s helped the company to become a global leader in mobile telecommunications.

These policy shifts facilitated by technology transfer offices sparked a boom in academic patenting and startups. As a result, academic startups have become a prominent engine of innovation, and pioneering universities have embraced their dual role as educators and entrepreneurs. This symbiotic approach attempts to leverage academic research for economic and social benefit while also generating revenues to fund future research.

The future will see even greater integration between academia and industry as universities actively cultivate ecosystems to translate ideas into impact. As this unfolds, maintaining scientific integrity and commitment to learning remains imperative.

Growing Socio-Economic Impact

So, as universities are increasingly adopting the role of innovation incubators and enterprise catalysts, their impact in the economy is growing. This is evident in the fact that the top 100 universities in the world that have been granted the most U.S. utility patents are all actively contributing to the startup ecosystem to a degree that significantly exceeds the average. Institutions such as Stanford, MIT, Oxford, and Cambridge are outstanding examples of academic entrepreneurship across the science and technology spectrum. They have given birth to literally thousands of startups that have transformed entire sectors and revolutionized our daily lives.

Stanford, for instance, is a hotbed of academic entrepreneurship, and its alumni have founded some of the most influential companies in Silicon Valley. A case in point is Google, which was founded by two Stanford students, Larry Page and Sergey Brin. The company has literally transformed the way we live and work, and it is hard to imagine a world without its search engine.

Another example of a Stanford-founded company that has had a major impact is Sun Microsystems. The company was founded by three Stanford graduates, Vinod Khosla, Andy Bechtolsheim, and Scott McNealy. Sun Microsystems revolutionized the computer world with its pioneering work in network computing. Its Network File System (NFS) set the stage for distributed computing, a precursor to today's cloud-based systems.

On the East Coast, the Massachusetts Institute of Technology (MIT) is another hugely potent force in academic entrepreneurship. One of its success stories is Moderna Therapeutics, which was co-founded by Professor Robert Langer. His laboratory has been the source of over 40 startups in areas as diverse as drug delivery systems and tissue engineering. One of these startups, Moderna, developed a groundbreaking mRNA vaccine for COVID-19 that was one of the first approved vaccines for the disease and helped change the course of the pandemic, saving countless lives in the process.

In the UK, academic institutions have become fertile grounds for startups, each nurturing a unique ecosystem of innovation. Take, for instance, the University of Oxford, which has seeded hundreds of startups that helped turn groundbreaking ideas into commercial realities. One of its most famous spin-offs, Oxford Nanopore Technologies—featured in our case study in Chapter 7—was born in Professor Hagan Bayley's laboratory within the university's Chemistry Department. This innovation revolutionized DNA sequencing, making it faster, more accessible, and even portable enough to be used aboard NASA's International Space Station (Brown et al., 2023).

Of course, academic entrepreneurship extends well beyond the borders of just Oxford. For example, the University of Cambridge, a long-standing academic competitor, has also nurtured an energetic startup environment, particularly prominent within the field of biotechnology. This is prominently observed in the vicinity known as Silicon Fen, a hotspot brimming with high-tech businesses, innovative startups, and avant-garde research facilities. A case in point is the pharmaceutical titan AstraZeneca, which has established a significant footprint at the Cambridge Biomedical Campus, capitalizing on the wealth of talent and innovative vigor in the region.

In a similar vein, Imperial College London has been a fertile ground for a large array of startups, notably within the clean-tech and health-tech sectors. An example is Bboxx, a startup born from the entrepreneurial spirit of Imperial College graduates, which has made considerable strides in the clean-tech industry by devising smart solar systems that offer affordable electricity in remote, off-grid regions in developing countries. On the health-tech front, DeepMind is a great example of an AI-driven global business. Starting its journey as an Imperial College spin-off, DeepMind has ascended to become a worldwide leader in artificial intelligence and machine learning, with its applications spanning areas as diverse as protein folding and healthcare improvement.

Beyond the UK, several European universities are actively bridging the gap between academic research and entrepreneurial ventures. The Swiss Federal Institute of Technology in Zurich, École Polytechnique Fédérale de Lausanne in Switzerland, and Technical University of Munich in Germany are pioneering leaders in this realm. And let's not forget the Max Planck Society in Germany, with its dozens of institutes contributing to a wide range of sectors, from biotech startups like Evotec and MorphoSys to exciting high-tech ventures in the area of quantum computing, such as IQM.

Each of these institutions exemplifies the transformative power of academic entrepreneurship, not only in generating economic value but also in catalyzing societal change. Their stories reveal how scientific discovery, when coupled with entrepreneurial spirit, can cross the boundaries of laboratories and transform the world.

But while these examples demonstrate how academic entrepreneurship, nourished by supportive universities and brilliant researchers, can yield innovations that change the world, the "translation" is far from straightforward. Indeed, transitioning from lab to market is a challenging journey—where we need to balance the cultures, expectations, and practicalities of both academia and business. This demands a shift in mindset and strategies for tackling issues related to funding, intellectual property, and successful commercialization.

As we explore the vibrant world of academic startups, envisioning their creation is akin to a complex dance set in a three-dimensional space. This space encompasses three intertwined spheres: the academic realm, where researchers secure funding; the commercial domain, focused on translating research into tangible products or services; and the financial arena, where investors seek profitable returns. For a spin-off to thrive, there must be a harmonious convergence of these spheres, orchestrated by those adept at navigating the myriad challenges that arise.

Yet, the choreography of this dance extends beyond mere mechanics. It is suffused with the human spirit—the tech transfer officer unraveling the intricacies of university technology transfer; the astute manager steering the venture towards strategic goals, weaving compelling narratives about the startup's potential, and showcasing financial savvy. A combination of varied skills underpins success. However, equally indispensable is passion. Fostering and scaling spin-out companies demands unwavering commitment. It's a path for the tenacious, those animated by their pioneering research and its latent potential. Absent this mix of skills and relentless drive, the specter of failure becomes all too real.

The Role of TTOs: Orchestrators of Innovation

Building on our discussion of the historical evolution of universities, we have seen how the modern institution has metamorphosed beyond its traditional educational and research-centric roots. Universities today are crucibles of innovation, fostering societal progress and economic dynamism. Within this milieu of knowledge synthesis and dissemination, Technology Transfer Offices

(TTOs) play a pivotal role, channeling academic breakthroughs into tangible real-world applications.

The narrative of academic startups isn't merely about commercializing an idea; it's a journey that involves multiple stages—from earmarking potential intellectual property (IP) to charting the course through the complex web of patents and licenses. Here, TTOs anchor the process in several critically important ways:

1. **Intellectual Property Navigation:** For every nascent academic startup, the commercial journey's first step is grasping the IP's inherent value. TTOs illuminate this path, discerning patent-worthy discoveries from those better shared through publications.

2. **Licensing and Contracts:** Once a prospective IP is earmarked, its protection is vital. TTOs excel here, crafting and finessing licenses that ensure alignment between the institution's goals and the aspirations of startups and investors.

3. **Connecting the Dots:** Groundbreaking academic insights need a conduit to the commercial world, often necessitating industry affiliations. TTOs bridge this gap, forging ties with industry counterparts, financiers, and other pivotal players.

4. **Mitigating Risks:** Any entrepreneurial venture is riddled with risks. When academia is at the heart of a startup, these risks are accentuated. TTOs, adept at navigating both the academic and commercial realms, are invaluable in anticipating and neutralizing these threats.

5. **Resource Allocation:** In academia-driven startups, resources are precious. TTOs adeptly guide resource allocation, pinpointing investment opportunities, suggesting worthy grants, and maximizing the value derived from constrained funds.

Academic startups light the path with their innovations, but TTOs are the bridges that span the chasm between the laboratory and the market. They shepherd promising technologies through the treacherous "Valley of Death" (which we'll be discussing next) where many promising innovations fail to reach commercialization. Indeed, these dedicated teams play a vital role in protecting intellectual property and smoothly facilitating the transfer of technology to the private sector.

Surviving the Cash Crunch: Trial By Fire

Transitioning from a conceptual stage to the marketplace is like navigating a tempest. One formidable challenge stands out: crossing the dreaded valley of death. This term, explored extensively in Chapter 7, symbolizes a startup's tenuous early phase—a defining "make or break" moment.

At this juncture, while the venture is still refining its offerings and vying for market space, reliable revenue streams are elusive. Thus, the venture's expenditure often outweighs its earnings, possibly foretelling an impending failure.

Here, startups are often shackled by stringent financial bounds. If they are unable to turn a profit soon, they may be forced to shut down. They need funds to sustain product evolution and market entry campaigns. And in the absence of tangible commercial momentum, investors are deterred. An incomplete grasp of market dynamics further exacerbates their challenges, hindering effective response strategies and curbing their chances of gaining significant market traction. The metaphorical "death" materializes – one more company in the heap of academic venture failures.

CASE STUDY: GOOGLE

The birth of Google, one of the most successful academic startups, can be traced back to a research project at Stanford University in the mid-1990s. Stanford Ph.D. candidates Larry Page and Sergey Brin embarked on a mission to organize the world's information, driven by the belief that this would universally enhance accessibility and usefulness.

(FIGURE 9: GOOGLE)

Their project, which aimed to develop a unique search algorithm, began in early 1996. The algorithm, initially called "Backrub" and later renamed "PageRank," proposed an innovative method of ranking web pages based on their relevance and importance. Unlike other search engines that ranked results based on the number of times the search term appeared on the page, PageRank determined a website's relevance by the number of pages, and the importance of those pages, that linked back to the original site.

This groundbreaking approach required considerable computational resources, causing Stanford's servers to crash repeatedly. The duo even built their own computer housing from LEGO to allow for additional hard drives.

Encouraged by their advisor, they transformed their research into a startup in 1998, initially running operations from their dorm rooms and later from a friend's garage in Menlo Park. Despite humble beginnings, Google rapidly gained traction. By the end of 1998, it was processing 500,000 queries per day, and in August 2004, the company went public, changing the course of the internet industry.

Highlights: Google's journey from an academic project to a tech giant reveals the extraordinary potential of academic startups. It exemplifies the transformative power of university research commercialization, demonstrating how it can birth industry-disrupting, globally impactful businesses. Additionally, the story underscores the crucial role universities play in fostering an environment conducive to innovative thinking, entrepreneurship, and the creation of new industries.

CHAPTER 5:
Bridging Two Worlds: Academia & Practice

The journey of an academic entrepreneur is best described as a voyage between two worlds, each with its own customs, practices, and languages. One is the land of academia with its focus on scholarly rigor, peer review, and the pursuit of knowledge. The other is the realm of entrepreneurship, characterized by speed, competition, practical application, and financial viability.

This dichotomy echoes two different debates concerning distinct "worlds" or "cultures" within and beyond academia. The first, which I've already touched upon earlier, was sparked by British scientist and novelist C.P. Snow, and refers to the divide within academia itself. In his "Two Cultures" argument, Snow posited that the academic and scientific community (scientists, researchers) and the literary or "humanities" community (philosophers, sociologists, literary critics) exist as two disparate cultures, often oblivious to the other's methods and practices.

The second perspective, brought forth by Andrew Van de Ven, considers academia as a distinct arena within the broader societal context. His model differentiates between two "modes of knowledge creation and application."

Mode 1 epitomizes the pursuit of academic research, characterized by methodological rigor, empirical validation, and firm theoretical foundations. Here, the quest for new knowledge is driven by curiosity and a commitment to the pursuit of truth. It embodies knowledge creation which is governed by a systematic process of investigation and validation. Academic research typically focuses on a long-term time horizon and values knowledge for its own sake. Validation relies on peer review and building incrementally on existing theories.

In contrast, Mode 2 knowledge creation occurs when academics collaborate with industry practitioners to solve practical real-world problems. It emphasizes application, action, and tangible results over rigor. Knowledge is seen as a means to an end rather than an end in itself. Validation relies on real-world impact and feedback. The time horizon is short-term and iterative. An example is a professor collaborating with a biotech firm to develop a new medical treatment.

The cultural differences between academia and industry are substantial. Academia prioritizes long-term, curiosity-driven research while business focuses on practical, results-driven approaches aimed at financial gain. Academic culture values peer-reviewed publications, debates at conferences, and tenure-track positions. Business culture emphasizes profitability, return on investment, market share growth, and flexibility. These very different mindsets, incentives, and measures of success can lead to tension and misunderstandings when collaborating across the academia-industry divide.

Bridging this gap requires empathy, open communication, and a willingness to find common ground. Academics can better understand business priorities like speed, efficiency, and profitability. Business professionals can better appreciate the cautious, rigorous approach of academia. Socializing each other on their respective cultures and mindsets is essential. Joint conferences, exchange programs, and informal relationship building opportunities help create this mutual understanding.

Some academics have successfully bridged these two worlds, acting as "boundary spanners" that facilitate effective collaboration. They act as interpreters and intermediaries between the languages and logics of academia and business. These bridge builders leverage skills like cultural awareness, adaptability, and emotional intelligence to enable productive partnerships.

There are also structured initiatives designed to connect academia and industry, such as university incubators and accelerators, industry sabbaticals, university partnership offices, and collaborative R&D projects. These programs create valuable exchange opportunities, foster relationships, and promote mutual understanding between academia and business.

The future will likely see even more integration between the two worlds, as the lines blur between basic and applied research and knowledge increasingly needs to traverse the boundary into application to maximally benefit society. Academic entrepreneurs will play an important role in this intersection, combining academic excellence with business acumen.

In my lectures and writings on the tension between "rigor and relevance," or the divide between academia and practice, I examine the unique "logics" that govern these two spheres (see Figure 10). I explore the nuances that delineate and define their different approaches to knowledge, collaboration, validation, and communication.

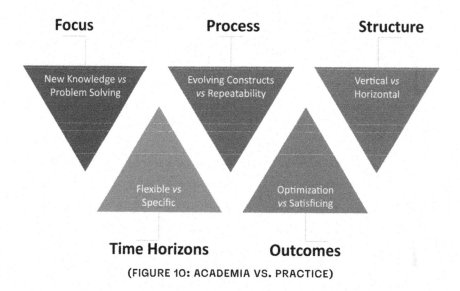

(FIGURE 10: ACADEMIA VS. PRACTICE)

Indeed, within the realm of academic entrepreneurship, these distinct paradigms converge and often create tensions. Academic entrepreneurs are, in essence, navigators at the confluence of two different "cultures" within academia (the sciences and the humanities) and two separate "paradigms" in the broader societal landscape (academia and industry). This dual existence can be a delicate balancing act, rife with challenges yet teeming with unique opportunities.

Take, for example, the management of Intellectual Property (IP), the subject of our next chapter. The academic culture typically fosters the open exchange of knowledge as its cardinal principle. The free flow of ideas isn't just deeply ingrained; it's also integral for peer review, validation, and the advancement of knowledge. Ideas aren't merely disseminated, but are subject to rigorous critique and open debate, thereby stretching the limits of our existing knowledge.

In stark contrast, the entrepreneurial paradigm often necessitates a degree of confidentiality until ideas are adequately protected. Within the competitive market environment, preserving a semblance of secrecy can tip the scales between success and failure. An untimely disclosure could derail an enterprise before it even sets sail, eroding its competitive edge and potential attractiveness to investors.

Furthermore, the language of academia stands in stark contrast to that of the business world. As an academic entrepreneur, you must expand your linguistic toolkit, shifting from the scholarly vernacular filled with scientific concepts and complex diagrams to a language that speaks to the business world—terms such as return on investment, customer traction, and scalability become integral to your dialogue.

Nowhere is this more evident or more crucial than in fundraising, a process that demands fluency in the language of investors. And it is not merely about understanding financial metrics; it's about articulating value propositions, demonstrating market traction, conveying potential scalability, and ultimately, communicating the business's potential to generate sustainable profits.

Understanding "investor speak" is more than an exercise in translation; it's akin to crossing a linguistic bridge into a distinct world, each side with its unique perspectives and expectations. It requires the academic entrepreneur to be bilingual, adept at both the meticulous precision of academic discourse and the persuasive clarity of entrepreneurial storytelling.

In academia, where deep tech startups are nurtured, the scholar-entrepreneur can take advantage of resources such as research facilities, faculty expertise, and student talent. However, the two dualities (that are certainly not mutually exclusive) can create tensions for academic entrepreneurs who must navigate between them. His or her challenge lies in maintaining academic integrity while evading potential conflicts of interest, skillfully managing the fine balance between intellectual quest of scholarly discourse and the pragmatic sphere of business. Viewed through the lens of paradox theory, these two domains may seem contradictory but are, in fact, interdependent, fostering a dynamic environment ripe for both conflict and synergy.

These tensions are not unique to this context; they resonate in scenarios where advanced technologies, like artificial intelligence (AI), are integrated into organizational settings. Consider, for instance, the adoption of AI in a corporate setting. As humans and AI co-exist, friction inevitably arises, not just between different types of AI, but also between artificial and human actors. To ensure the successful assimilation of these technologies in the workplace, organizational members must adapt to this new co-existence or find innovative ways to alleviate the tension.

The same principles hold true within academic entrepreneurship. Academic entrepreneurs must learn to not only coexist, but also prosper amidst the contrasting demands of academia and the business world. "Boundary spanners" or "knowledge brokers" become critical in facilitating this transformation. These intermediaries help translate academic knowledge into practical business applications, fostering a productive dialogue between academia and industry, and paving the path for research-driven innovations.

In this light, Van de Ven's concept of "getting more parts on the table" stands as an appropriate metaphor for this process. Academic entrepreneurs, by virtue of their unique position, infuse their ventures with diverse perspectives, insights, and experiences. They meld academic rigor with entrepreneurial relevance, enriching their entrepreneurial journey.

Of course, reconciling the apparent paradoxes of academic entrepreneurship goes beyond conflict resolution or mere compromise. It involves creating a vibrant synthesis between the worlds of academia and business, transforming inherent tension into a dynamic interplay that fuels innovation. As a result, academic entrepreneurs, with the guidance of their mentors, may emerge not merely as innovators but as paradox navigators, who steer their ventures through the intertwined domains of scholarly pursuit and entrepreneurial action.

CASE STUDY: OXBOTICA

Oxbotica, a pioneering autonomous vehicle software startup, spun out from pioneering research at the University of Oxford. The company develops AI-powered software that gives vehicles full autonomy by enabling them to perceive and navigate their surroundings without human assistance.

The company was founded in 2014 by two world-renowned experts in robotics and artificial intelligence, Professors Paul Newman and Ingmar Posner. The company was born out of Oxford University's Mobile Robotics Group, and it has since become a global leader in the autonomous vehicle industry.

(FIGURE 11: OXBOTICA)

Challenges and opportunities
Oxbotica's founders faced significant challenges when they transitioned from academia to the business world. They had to create a viable business model, secure funding, protect their IP, and translate their advanced robotics and artificial intelligence research into a marketable product.

To address these challenges, the founders used their academic expertise to their advantage while adopting entrepreneurial strategies. Their deep understanding of autonomous systems helped them create a unique value proposition. They opted for a "software-only" business model, focusing on universal autonomy applicable across sectors. This decision reflected their nuanced understanding of both the technology and the market.

Oxbotica's story underlines the delicate dance between academia and business. The founders successfully bridged the two worlds, securing substantial investments, including £14m in Series A funding. Today, Oxbotica is a global leader in autonomous vehicle technology, working with major automakers and logistics companies worldwide.

Technology

Oxbotica's software uses multiple sensors like lidar, radar, and cameras integrated with deep learning algorithms to build a comprehensive model of the vehicle's environment and make navigation decisions. The company's technology is highly scalable and can be adapted to a wide range of vehicles and operating environments.

Commercial traction

Oxbotica has raised over $100 million in funding from investors like bp ventures, Oxford Sciences Innovation, Tencent, and others. The company has partnerships with companies like bp, Addison Lee, AppliedEV, and IMS to test and deploy its technology.

In 2021, Oxbotica piloted the first fully autonomous vehicle passenger shuttle in Europe, deployed in a mixed pedestrian and vehicular public space in Oxford. In 2022, Oxbotica secured regulatory approval to publicly trial fully driverless vehicles on UK roads without safety drivers, a significant milestone.

Competitive landscape

Oxbotica competes with other major players in the autonomous vehicle industry, including Waymo, Cruise, Argo AI, and Motional. However, Oxbotica differentiates itself through its focus on software. The company's software can be integrated into a wide range of vehicles and operating environments, giving it a competitive advantage.

Challenges

The commercialization of autonomous vehicles faces a number of challenges, including safety, regulatory approvals, and user trust. Oxbotica is addressing these challenges by developing highly safe and reliable autonomous systems, working closely with regulators to ensure compliance, and educating the public about the benefits of autonomous vehicles.

Highlights: Oxbotica's story is a testament to the power of academic research and the potential for entrepreneurship to drive innovation. The company's founders were able to use their academic expertise to create a successful business, and they are now helping to shape the future of transportation.

CHAPTER 6:

Exploitation of University Intellectual Property

In an era where academic entrepreneurship is rapidly transforming academic insights into market-ready products and services, the emphasis on intellectual property (IP) has never been greater. This transition, where academia assumes roles beyond traditional teaching and research, is backed by governments and policymakers globally. As the world progressively shifts towards a knowledge-based economy, IP becomes an indispensable tool for universities aiming to harness their innovative capabilities.

Intellectual property, encapsulating elements such as patents, copyrights, trademarks, and trade secrets, safeguards inventions, discoveries, and creative endeavors. By effectively navigating the intricacies of IP, universities can monetize their innovations through licensing agreements, patent sales, and the creation of spin-off companies. Furthermore, IP offers universities the potential to foster new industries, address global challenges, and contribute to societal advancement.

Historically, the U.S. pioneered the reinforcement of academic IP through the Bayh-Dole Act of 1980. As I've previously noted, this landmark legislation empowered universities, nonprofit research institutions, and small businesses to retain IP rights for inventions stemming from federally-funded research, sparking a surge in patent applications and subsequent technological commercialization.

Of course, understanding the vast realm of IP is essential for successfully navigating the process. Patent laws, an essential subset of IP, vary significantly across countries. The way in which inventions are disclosed is especially crucial. Indeed, mishandling discussions with external entities can inadvertently forfeit patenting rights. Notably, while the U.S. and U.K. have similar IP laws, protecting your product or brand through trademarks is also highly advisable. Without these protective measures, you risk others capitalizing on your ideas.

Furthermore, understanding the distinctions between patents, copyrights, trade secrets, and other IP aspects is imperative for protecting and commercializing one's innovations. The Chartered Institute of Management Accountants (CIMA) is one of the most vocal proponents of the need to "ring-fence" innovative ideas, pointing out that new concepts can be protected for years before entering the public domain—which requires a willingness to view the modest expense involved as a wise investment.

Navigating the patenting and development process can be complex. While patents are often seen as an invaluable asset, they can also have inherent limitations. They can be financially draining, challenging to uphold, and vulnerable to larger entities that can exhaust a university's resources in litigation. Interestingly, while certain universities gain recognition for their spin-offs, their most notable successes may arise from copyrights (often related to software developments) rather than patents.

The Triple Helix Model

The Triple Helix Model has emerged as a potent strategy to ignite the flame of innovation, commercialization, and economic development. At its core, it embodies the harmonious collaboration between three pivotal entities: universities, government, and industry.

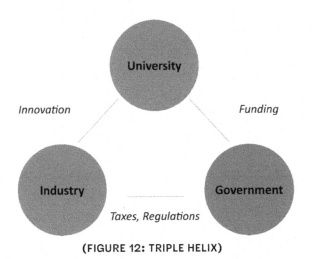

(FIGURE 12: TRIPLE HELIX)

In the Triple Helix framework, universities, once siloed within academic pursuits, evolve as epicenters of tangible innovation. Their research and advancements have the potential not only to spark new industries and employment opportunities but also to address paramount societal challenges ranging from healthcare solutions to environmental conservation. However, the fruits of such academic endeavors are susceptible to appropriation. It's here that the need for a robust IP strategy becomes paramount. By protecting the intellectual assets stemming from universities, the innovation process can be both rewarding and sustainable.

Europe's nuanced approach, transitioning from initial hesitation to a staunch commitment to "valorization" or the commercialization of academic knowledge, is a testament to this paradigm. Programs such as Horizon Europe (2021-2027), with its staggering €100 billion funding pool, underscore the European commitment to champion the Triple Helix Model. These initiatives aim to galvanize academic entrepreneurship and push the frontiers of innovation. However, without a sturdy bulwark of IP protection, the valorization process remains vulnerable, potentially negating the gains of commercialization.

The geometry of the Triple Helix Model, often depicted as a triangle, serves as a symbolic representation of its essence. Each vertex stands for a stakeholder—universities offer knowledge and research capabilities (safeguarded through IP), the government lays down the policy groundwork and infuses funding, and industries act as the gateway to market dynamics, capital, and scalability. This synergy creates an ecosystem where innovation thrives and economies flourish.

This trinity reinforces the imperative to address societal challenges while pioneering new industries and technologies. As we pivot into an era where knowledge holds unprecedented value, the Triple Helix Model emerges as a keystone in fostering innovation, economic growth, and redefining the university's societal role.

Undoubtedly, at the heart of valorization pulses intellectual property. It's the lifeline that ensures the fruits of innovation remain protected and, in turn, commercially viable:

(FIGURE 13: FORMS OF IP)

- **Patents**: Guarding the invention blueprints for a stipulated timeframe, patents ensure the inventor's rights remain unchallenged. Especially for tangible innovations, patents provide a shield, ensuring returns on hefty R&D investments.

- **Trade Secrets**: This realm of IP cocoons proprietary business insights, processes, and technologies. Keeping competitors at bay, trade secrets can endure indefinitely, as long as confidentiality remains unbreached.

- **Copyrights**: Autonomously safeguarding creative works, copyrights ensure that the creator's intellectual expressions remain inviolable, providing a legal recourse against unsanctioned duplications.

- **Trademarks**: Beyond mere logos or symbols, trademarks encapsulate brand identity. They become signifiers of trust, quality, and reliability in the marketplace.

The potency of IP within the Triple Helix Model cannot be overstated. As we explore the nuances of this synergy, we transition into the pivotal strategic choices academic founders must navigate when it comes to IP protection.

Strategic Choices around IP

Safeguarding intellectual property is fundamental in academic entrepreneurship. Your IP strategy is shaped by the uniqueness of the invention, your startup's business model, and market dynamics as well as a host of other considerations. Le's examine each form of protection:

Patents: Patents provide exclusive rights to an invention for a limited period, typically 20 years from the filing date. Especially crucial for tangible innovations like pharmaceuticals, patents shield against the unauthorized replication of your invention. However, the patent process isn't straightforward, and several key factors need to be well understood before making the relevant choices.

> **Drafting and Filing**: Begin with a detailed patent application, illustrating your invention's uniqueness and applicability. Enlist the expertise of a patent attorney to ensure the language is precise and all-encompassing.
>
> **Jurisdictional Choices**: Once your patent application is ready, decide on the jurisdictions where you seek protection. Not all patents require global coverage, but consider where your potential markets and competitors are.
>
> **Patent Landscaping**: Conduct a thorough patent landscape analysis. This provides an overview of existing patents in your domain, helping identify potential competition, collaboration opportunities, or even gaps in the current market.
>
> **Defensive vs. Offensive Strategy**: Not all patents are filed with the intent to commercialize. Some serve as defensive strategies, preventing competitors from entering specific market areas. Conversely,

an offensive strategy seeks to commercialize or license the patent for revenue.

Trade Secrets: Ideal for proprietary processes or technologies hard to reverse-engineer. Unlike patents, they don't expire but require internal measures to ensure confidentiality. Decide early if the potential longevity of a trade secret outweighs the temporary protection but public disclosure of a patent.

Copyrights and Trademarks: These protect creative works and brand identity respectively. While copyrights are automatic, trademarks require a formal application. As an academic founder, understanding the distinction helps in cases where your startup's brand or educational content needs protection.

So, beyond individual IP choices, consider how they integrate. Take a holistic approach. For instance, software startups might rely on a blend of patents (for unique algorithms), copyrights (for code), and trade secrets (for proprietary processes).

As the world of IP is intricate and complex, Technology Transfer Offices (TTOs) and patent law firms are vital allies. They can guide you through IP registration, help navigate potential pitfalls, and, when needed, defend against infringements.

From Theory to Practice

While the realm of IP can appear daunting, it's essential to view it as an enabler. By protecting your intellectual assets, you solidify your startup's market position and potential for growth.

Consider Spotify's evolution from academic research in Sweden to a global enterprise. This journey exemplified the intricate dance between patents, trade secrets, and copyrights. Balancing academic commitments and entrepreneurship was challenging but ultimately rewarding.

Universities today grapple with the dual role of disseminating knowledge and fostering innovation. Academic founders, therefore, need to tread cautiously.

While IP protection is crucial, it's equally important to share and grow knowledge for the broader benefit.

In upcoming chapters, we'll dive deeper, providing academic founders with tactical insights and actionable advice. But before that, let's explore Genentech's journey, offering a lens into the successful leveraging of university-generated IP, setting the stage for a global biotech revolution.

CASE STUDY: GENENTECH

Genentech, widely acknowledged as a cornerstone of the global biotechnology sector, was originally an academic startup. In the mid-1970s, Herbert Boyer of the University of California, San Francisco, and Stanley Cohen from Stanford University made a huge scientific breakthrough. They developed recombinant DNA technology, a method that enabled the combination of DNA from different species.

(FIGURE 14: GENENTECH)

Genentech's trajectory serves as an exemplar of successful university intellectual property exploitation. It emphasizes the potential of cutting-edge academic research, the importance of strategic partnerships, and the role of effective IP management. The company's journey underscores how these elements, when expertly combined, can drive the success of academic startups, leading to groundbreaking innovations that revolutionize industries and significantly improve human health.

One of the key factors in Genentech's success has been its ability to effectively commercialize its academic IP through strategic partnerships with major pharmaceutical companies, such as Roche. They also bolstered their capabilities by investing heavily in clinical development and marketing.

Genentech's use of generative AI to identify and develop new targeted therapies is another example of how the company is leveraging its IP to create innovative products that meet the needs of patients. Generative AI is a powerful tool that can be used to screen large numbers of molecules for potential therapeutic activity. This can help to accelerate the drug discovery process and to identify new drug candidates that are more likely to be successful in clinical trials.

Genentech's use of generative AI is also helping to improve the marketing of its targeted therapies. The company is using AI to develop personalized marketing campaigns that target patients who are most likely to benefit from its products. This is helping to ensure that the right medicines are getting to the right patients.

Genentech's success demonstrates the importance of effective IP management for academic startups. By protecting and commercializing its IP, Genentech has been able to develop and bring to market innovative products that are making a real difference in the lives of patients.

As of today, Genentech, a member of the Roche Group, boasts a market capitalization in excess of $200 billion. The company employs more than 13,000 people, and its products are used to treat conditions in numerous therapeutic areas, including oncology, immunology, and neuroscience.

Highlights: Genentech's trajectory serves as an exemplar of successful university intellectual property exploitation. It emphasizes the potential of cutting-edge academic research, the importance of strategic partnerships, and the role of effective IP management. The company's journey underscores how these elements, when combined, can drive the success of academic startups, leading to groundbreaking innovations that revolutionize industries and significantly improve human health.

CHAPTER 7:
Traversing the Valley of Death

The journey of an academic startup is certainly a challenging one, but it can also be incredibly rewarding. It is a tale woven from threads of resilience, audacity, and aspiration. One of the most important milestones in this journey is the "valley of death," a period when the startup is faced with a number of operational challenges, such as limited funding and resources.

During the valley of death, the startup has typically established a prototype or proof-of-concept, but it is not yet generating revenue. This can be a difficult period for the startup, but it is also a critical one. Startups that are able to successfully navigate the valley of death are well on their way to becoming successful businesses.

As touched upon in Chapter 4, particularly when defining Technology Readiness Levels (TRLs) as a framework for evaluating technology maturity, this phase typically corresponds to TRLs 4-6. At this stage, the startup has successfully established a prototype or proof-of-concept but also finds itself grappling with a variety of operational costs."

These costs aren't merely confined to obvious expenditures like salaries, office space, and equipment maintenance, but also include critical support services such as basic accounting and legal counsel. These services, though not directly contributing to product development, are vital to the administrative and legal functioning of the startup.

What is more, the startup is likely to be facing ongoing costs associated with research and development as well as marketing and customer acquisition. And let's not overlook potential outlays for regulatory compliance and patent filing fees. For startups operating in international markets, costs related to tax filings, and possibly transfer pricing, in various jurisdictions may also become relevant.

This is a phase where the startup's "burn rate"—the rate at which it's depleting its capital over time—becomes an essential metric to monitor. Without steady revenue streams, the venture is heavily dependent on seed capital or investments, as the prospect of organic growth remains elusive during this phase. Navigating this financial tightrope is a critical part of surviving the valley of death, and it underlines the importance of prudent fiscal management for any academic startup.

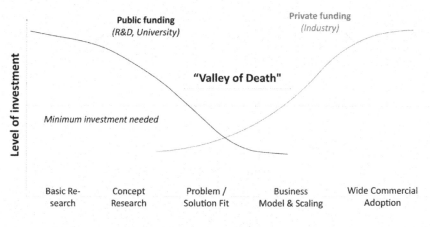

(FIGURE 15: THE VALLEY OF DEATH)

So, in this precarious limbo, the startup's technological groundwork has been laid, but the road to commercial viability is still clouded by numerous uncertainties—ranging from market acceptance and regulatory compliance to funding constraints. The challenge, thus, extends beyond merely reaching technical milestones; it requires developing a compelling value proposition that resonates with market demands and investor expectations.

Regrettably, a significant proportion of startups fail to navigate this chasm, succumbing to diverse challenges such as liquidity crises, insufficient market traction, or strategic missteps like poor planning or lack of prioritization. This phase can be treacherous, with even minor missteps potentially leading to failure if robust support structures are not in place or if fears manage to dampen the entrepreneurial spirit.

Understanding the Four Phases

The four-phase model of startup development, as well as the valley of death, provide insightful perspectives on a startup's journey from its inception to a profitable business. While not perfectly correlated, these concepts jointly highlight the strategic, operational, and financial challenges that startups face. Recognizing these stages can provide startups with a roadmap for their journey, helping them understand how to navigate their venture through the toughest phase—the valley of death.

It's crucial to underscore, however, that navigating the valley of death can be skillfully undertaken, emerging on the other side more robust and better focused. The sobering reality, indeed, is that whilst the odds tend to not favor a successful traversal, with a methodical approach the odds become much better. This amplifies the importance of resilience, strategic acumen, and, often, institutional support.

Although the valley of death is commonly associated with TRL 4-6, where a startup is developing a proto-type and attempting to achieve market traction, the journey through the valley can stretch across different stages of a start-up's lifecycle as outlined by Ritter and Pedersen (HBR 2022).

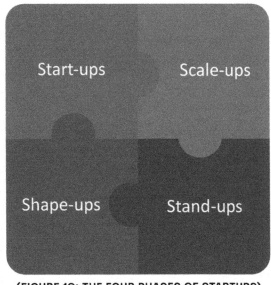

(FIGURE 16: THE FOUR PHASES OF STARTUPS)

The "Shape-ups" and "Stand-ups" phases align broadly with the earlier part of the valley of death. Here, startups are developing their prototypes and starting to seek initial funding, with the lurking financial risk of the valley on the horizon.

As ventures move into the "Start-ups" phase, they find themselves well inside the valley, grappling with cash flow issues, market validation, and user acquisition. It's at this critical juncture where many startups falter, unable to maintain the momentum needed to reach the other side.

However, those that manage to persevere begin to emerge from the valley as they transition into the "Scale-ups" phase. Having established a degree of product-market fit and secured a reliable revenue stream, these ventures focus on scaling their operations, increasing their market share, and, ideally, turning a profit.

While the four-phase model and the concept of the valley of death don't map directly onto each other, they offer complementary perspectives on a startup's journey. The valley of death highlights the financial perils startups face, while the four-phase model sheds light on strategic and operational challenges. Together, they provide a holistic understanding of a startup's path from idea generation to profitable growth.

Shape-ups: In this initial phase, startups are busy shaping their ideas, technologies, and potential business models. They may still be primarily based in an academic setting, and their ideas might still be in the formative stages. This phase overlaps with the earlier TRLs where ideas are taken from concepts to initial prototypes. It is here that the looming valley of death starts to take form as startups scramble to shape a viable concept that will attract funding and market interest.

Stand-ups: Startups in this phase stand up and begin to take steps towards becoming an operational business. They might start seeking seed funding, begin building their teams, and further develop their prototypes. Here, startups are standing on the edge of the valley, looking across to the other side. The challenge lies in building a sturdy bridge—a viable business model—that will carry them across.

Start-ups: During this stage, the startups have made their initial leap into the market. They are in the midst of the valley, grappling with issues such as cash flow, user acquisition, and market validation. They are working tirelessly to establish product-market fit and generate enough revenue to stay afloat. This phase corresponds to the heart of the valley of death, where the startup's resilience is tested, and where strategic decision-making becomes critical for survival.

Scale-ups: In the final phase, the startup begins to emerge from the valley. They have achieved a certain degree of product-market fit, established a customer base, and generated a reliable revenue stream. Now, they're focusing on scaling up their operations, increasing their market share, and becoming profitable. The startup has successfully traversed the valley and is now focusing on growth and scaling.

We've now painted a detailed picture of a typical startup's trajectory, and explored the concept of product-market fit—a critical milestone all startups aim for. This achievement is not merely a marker of progress, but often a key determinant of whether a startup can cross the valley of death and evolve into a thriving, sustainable business.

It also sets the stage for the next chapter, where we will discuss a crucial component of a startup's journey—crafting a robust Go-to-Market Strategy. This strategy builds upon the product-market fit, offering a roadmap on how to effectively deliver the product to the customer, achieving competitive advantage, and maintaining sustainable growth.

Achieving Product-Market Fit

Product-market fit is reached when your startup's offering is in such demand that a substantial portion of users would express significant disappointment if they lost access to it, a test suggested by Sean Ellis, founder of GrowthHackers. This pivotal achievement underscores that your product has become not just a nice-to-have, but an essential solution in the eyes of your customers.

(FIGURE 17: PRODUCT-MARKET FIT. ADAPTED FROM D. OLSEN)

Throughout the four phases of startup evolution, the pursuit of product-market fit remains a constant theme. It starts as an idea to be shaped, evolves into a hypothesis to be tested, becomes a goal to be achieved, and finally, a competitive advantage to be maintained and enhanced.

Here are four steps that might guide you towards achieving a solid fit:

1. **Identify Your Target Customer**: Understand your customer. Develop an in-depth customer profile or persona, understand their needs, their pain points, and how your product or service can address them.

2. **Clarify Your Value Proposition**: Clearly articulate the unique value your product or service offers to your target customer. How does it solve their problem? How is it better or different from existing solutions?

3. **Test and Validate**: Implement the Build-Measure-Learn feedback loop. Develop a minimum viable product (MVP), measure

how it performs in the market, learn from the feedback, and iterate accordingly.

4. **Iterate Until You Find Fit**: Based on the feedback, refine and adjust your product or service, your target customer, or your value proposition. Repeat this process until you find the right fit between your product and the market.

Of course, product-market fit isn't a one-off milestone but an ongoing endeavor. It requires a continuous commitment to learning, iterating, and adapting as markets evolve and customer preferences shift. Surviving the valley of death is just the beginning; a successful startup thrives beyond it by constantly realigning its strategies to meet the demands of the market.

With this understanding of the importance of achieving product-market fit, we now turn our attention to a case study that will illustrate how Oxford Nanopore successfully traversed the valley, and went on to revolutionize the bio-tech sector.

CASE STUDY: OXFORD NANOPORE

Oxford Nanopore Technologies (ONT) is a prime example of a company that has not only successfully traversed the valley of death but went on to become globally dominant player. Founded in 2005, ONT pioneered nanopore sequencing technology, a revolutionary new way to sequence DNA. ONT's sequencers have had a significant impact on the field of genomics, enabling new discoveries in cancer research, infectious disease surveillance, and agricultural biotechnology.

(FIGURE 18: OXFORD NANOPORE)

Nanopore Sequencing Technology

Nanopore sequencing works by passing DNA molecules through a protein nanopore. As the DNA molecule passes through the nanopore, it creates a unique electrical signal that is characteristic of the DNA sequence. This signal is then decoded to produce the DNA sequence.

Nanopore sequencing has several advantages over traditional sequencing methods, such as Sanger sequencing and Illumina sequencing. Nanopore sequencing is faster, more affordable, and can sequence longer DNA molecules. Additionally, nanopore sequencing can be used to sequence DNA in real-time, making it ideal for applications such as rapid pathogen detection and in-field genome sequencing.

ONT Product Offerings and Use Cases

ONT offers a range of nanopore sequencing products, including the MinION, GridION, PromethION, and Flongle.

- MinION: The MinION is a portable DNA sequencer that can be used in a variety of settings, including laboratories, field sites, and even space. The MinION is ideal for applications such as rapid pathogen detection, in-field genome sequencing, and environmental monitoring.

- GridION: The GridION is a medium-throughput DNA sequencer that is ideal for research and clinical applications. The GridION can be used to sequence DNA from a variety of sources, including human blood, saliva, and tissue samples.

- PromethION: The PromethION is a high-throughput DNA sequencer that is ideal for research and clinical applications. The PromethION can be used to sequence DNA from a variety of sources, including human blood, saliva, tissue samples, and microbial cultures.

- Flongle: The Flongle is a fast, small DNA sequencer that is ideal for rapid prototyping and point-of-care testing. The Flongle can be used to sequence DNA from a variety of sources, including human blood, saliva, and tissue samples.

ONT's products are used in a wide range of applications, including:

- Human genomics: ONT's products are used to sequence human genomes for research and clinical purposes. For example, ONT's sequencers have been used to identify new genetic variants associated with diseases such as cancer and autism.

- Microbial genomics: ONT's products are used to sequence microbial genomes to identify and characterize pathogens, track the spread of disease, and develop new antimicrobial treatments. For example, ONT's sequencers were used to sequence the genome of the Ebola virus during the 2013-2016 outbreak.

- Agricultural genomics: ONT's products are used to sequence the genomes of crops and livestock to improve crop yields, develop disease-resistant varieties, and track the movement of genetically modified organisms.

- Environmental genomics: ONT's products are used to sequence the genomes of organisms in the environment to study biodiversity, monitor ecosystem health, and track the spread of invasive species.

Now applying the "death valley curve" phase model to the company's initial development and beyond, we can see some key transitions:

The Shape-Up Phase
Throughout the shape-up phase, the founders honed their core technology, nanopore sequencing. Recognizing the technology's potential to democratize DNA sequencing, they developed a business model based on a compelling value proposition: making DNA sequencing portable, affordable, and real-time.

Their first product, the MinION—a pocket-sized DNA sequencer—was a tangible embodiment of this value proposition. The MinION could be used in a lab, in the field, and even in space, opening up genomic science to a wider array of users.

The Stand-Up Phase
Entering the stand-up phase, Oxford Nanopore faced skepticism and resistance from a market dominated by established players like Illumina. However, they persisted in proving their technology's viability.

They established strategic partnerships with academic and research institutions and launched an early-access program, enabling scientists to beta test the MinION. This strategy not only increased their credibility but also created a community of users providing essential feedback, contributing to the product's development and broader market acceptance.

Surviving Challenges

With the public launch of MinION in 2014, Oxford Nanopore entered the start-up phase. Despite the product's innovative design and affordability, they faced criticism about the accuracy of their sequencing technology.

Rather than backing down, Oxford Nanopore reinforced its commitment to its vision. They continuously improved the accuracy and reliability of their sequencers, launching new chemistry updates and improved software tools to address the scientific community's concerns.

Scaling Up and Beyond

By the time it reached the scale-up phase, Oxford Nanopore had proven its critics wrong. It expanded its product range to cater to a variety of sequencing needs, introducing the high-throughput PromethION sequencer, medium-throughput GridION, and fast, small Flongle. This diversification strategy cemented its market position.

In 2021, Oxford Nanopore went public, marking a significant milestone in its journey. Having successfully navigated the valley of death, the company continues to innovate and expand the boundaries of genomics with a robust product range and a growing global customer base.

Highlights: Oxford Nanopore's story illuminates the path through the valley of death for academic startups. Their journey underscores the importance of tenacity, strategic partnerships, continuous learning, and unwavering commitment to delivering on their value proposition.

CHAPTER 8:
Crafting a GTM Strategy: Key Building Blocks

In the preceding chapter, we discussed the valley of death, a phase in a startup's journey fraught with financial, technical, and operational hurdles. This phase signifies the transition from research and development—often supported by grants or academic institutions—to the commercialization of a revenue-generating product. Many startups stumble here, struggling to bridge the gap between initial funding to a point where they either become self-sustaining or attract substantial investment.

Towards the chapter's end, we touched upon "product-market fit." This pivotal moment occurs when a startup's offering starts to satisfy a notable market demand, reflecting its alignment with the genuine needs and desires of its target audience; not what we think they want, but what they demonstrate they want through their actions. Achieving this fit isn't just a milestone; it's a strong indicator of a startup's capability to serve its audience effectively, hinting at a successful emergence from the challenging "valley."

However, coming up with a product that can meet market demand is just the initial step. What follows is the crucial task of successfully introducing it to the market. The goal is to ensure that it not only finds its intended audience but also achieves significant market traction—affirming the venture's potential for long-term viability.

This progression brings us to the concept of the Go-To-Market (GTM) strategy. A well-structured GTM strategy, rooted in the foundation of an appealing product, provides a roadmap to solidify its market presence and foster growth.

In essence, while creating a product that aligns with potential market demand is foundational, the real challenge lies ahead. The next pivotal phase is ensuring that it is effectively introduced, reaches its target audience, and secures real market traction. A robust strategy, underpinned by a strong product foundation, outlines the steps to ensure that it reaches customers, gains traction in the market, and propels the venture's growth.

So, a GTM strategy is essentially a roadmap detailing how a product will penetrate the market effectively. It addresses pivotal questions such as:

- What is the offering (*product*)?
- Why would customers want it (*value*)?
- Who are the target customers (*target market*)?
- How will they be reached (*channels*)?
- What should be the pricing strategy (*price*)?
- How do we know our strategy is working (*KPIs*)?

What is Strategy?

Before examining the intricacies of crafting a GTM strategy, it's essential to first define what "strategy" is. At its core, strategy is about making informed choices that position a company to achieve its objectives. It provides a coherent and integrated framework that translates into a long-term plan, taking into account the organization's strengths, weaknesses, opportunities, and threats.

This definition emphasizes the significance of making informed, deliberate choices backed by evidence. A sound strategy isn't about trying everything in sight; it's about pinpointing the most promising initiatives and executing them methodically and with precision. Thus, strategy is as much about what we actively choose to pursue as it is about what we consciously decide NOT to.

A useful framework that underscores this idea is the "strategic choice cascade" introduced by Professor Roger Martin in collaboration with AG Lafley, the former CEO of Procter & Gamble. In their book *Playing to Win: How Strategy Really Works*, they outline five critical components for developing a solid strategy:

1. **Winning Aspiration:** The overarching goal or vision that an organization aspires to achieve.

2. **Where-to-Play:** Choices about which markets or segments the organization will target.

3. **How-to-Win:** The unique value proposition or approach that differentiates the organization from competitors.

4. **Must-Have Capabilities:** The essential skills or competencies required to execute the strategy effectively.

5. **Enabling Management Systems:** The internal processes and structures that support and drive the strategy forward.

A comprehensive approach to strategy weaves these components together, ensuring it's actionable, adaptable, and unified. Indeed, it's crucial to recognize that strategies aren't fixed plans; they're dynamic guides to decisions, where execution plays a pivotal role and exhibit a number of shared characteristics:

- **Clarity:** They are easy to understand and communicate.

- **Actionability:** They provide specific guidance for decision-making.

- **Realism:** They are grounded in an accurate assessment of the organization's capabilities and the external environment.

- **Adaptability:** They can evolve in response to changing circumstances.

Creating and Capturing Value

For every new venture, crafting a robust strategy is rooted in establishing a well-articulated business model. This model serves as the blueprint detailing how a company creates, delivers, and captures value. It's composed of nine foundational building blocks, ranging from customer segments to key activities and partnerships.

For academic ventures, especially those that are tech-driven, Dr. Najmaei's "core-periphery model" offers a useful perspective (Najmaei, 2018). This model suggests that academically driven ventures should be built around a robust technological core, complemented by a flexible marketing strategy. This combination allows for disruption while maintaining adaptability to shifting market conditions.

The main insight from this in business model terms is that technology-driven ventures stand a better chance to succeed if they are built around a scientific core that forms the basis of the value proposition, but they remain flexible in how they market and sell the product. This way, the offering is less likely to be easily replicated by competitors.

This strategic approach aligns closely with the product leadership strategy, one of the three strategies detailed in *The Discipline of Market Leaders* by Michael Treacy and Fred Wiersema. The product leadership model emphasizes creating and delivering top-tier, innovative products that stand out from the competition. It's a strategy often embraced by high-tech ventures, leveraging their technological prowess to craft truly disruptive products.

Product Leadership

(FIGURE 19: THE 3 DISCIPLINES)

Beyond the science or technology core, the flexible marketing periphery provides avenues for the venture to market and sell its products or services. This might involve diverse channels such as direct sales, online marketing, or partnerships with other businesses.

So, the core-periphery concept emphasizes a blend of a robust technological core with a flexible marketing or operational periphery—a combination that empowers technology ventures to be both disruptive and adaptable. They can pioneer new technologies or business models while concurrently adjusting to evolving market dynamics and consumer demands.

Examples of companies exemplifying the core-periphery model include:

- **Tesla**: At its foundation, Tesla boasts an advanced electric powertrain technology, a marked shift from conventional automotive engineering. This highly innovative core offers a sustainable alternative to gasoline engines, complemented by a direct-to-customer sales model. Eschewing the traditional dealership system, Tesla has the agility to modify its sales tactics, inaugurate showrooms at strategic junctures, and even facilitate online sales. Such adaptability enables Tesla to swiftly respond to market fluctuations, regulatory shifts, and evolving consumer preferences.

- **Genentech**: Central to the company's value proposition is its commitment to pioneering biotechnology for drug development. Their novel approach to drug discovery, rooted in recombinant DNA technology, distinguishes it in the field. Yet, its marketing and sales strategies remain malleable, often forming alliances with larger pharmaceutical companies and adapting to the constantly changing healthcare industry.

- **23andMe**: The company's cornerstone is its genetic testing technology, granting individuals insights into their lineage and potential health risks. While this technological core is steadfast, 23andMe's marketing strategies have evolved, transitioning from ancestry revelations to health predispositions, and even forging alliances with pharmaceutical giants for research.

- **Moderna**: Moderna's essence is encapsulated in its messenger RNA (mRNA) technology platform, instrumental in the swift formulation of a COVID-19 vaccine. While their scientific prowess is significant, their approach to partnerships and global distribution epitomizes the flexible periphery, adeptly navigating global demands and regulatory complexities.

These companies highlight that while a technological core can carve out a highly competitive niche, nimbleness in marketing and solid partnerships can greatly enhance market penetration as a vital yet complementary (peripheral) capability.

As technological breakthroughs continue to shape the global economy, such a product-centric approach is gaining prominence and is poised to be a dominant strategy for academic startups.

The Business Model Canvas: Mapping the Strategy

Building on a foundational understanding of how the venture will create and capture value, the Business Model Canvas, designed by Alexander Osterwalder and Yves Pigneur (Osterwalder, 2010), offers a pragmatic visual tool to crystallize and fine-tune a strategic direction. It is a highly useful framework for structuring your conversation around the choices to be made for each building block.

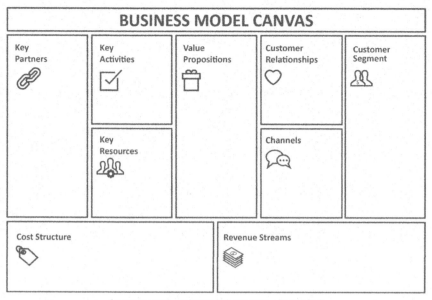

(FIGURE 20: BUSINESS MODEL CANVAS)

Covering nine pivotal elements—from customer segmentation to cost structures – the canvas is a holistic overview of a venture's strategic underpinnings. It's not just a tool for representation; it's an instrument for introspection. Startups, especially academic ones with their complex core-periphery structure, can use this canvas in internal workshops and strategy discussions. It enables them to delineate their value proposition, identify key stakeholders, map out revenue streams, and generally follow a logical structure for the key set of crucial choices that need to be made.

While the Business Model Canvas covers a wide array of key facets of a venture's strategic choice spectrum, it's not exhaustive. It offers a snapshot of the key components you need to consider without going into granular detail on each. Nonetheless, it provides both a starting point and a continually evolving guide, which should be updated as your startup grows, your market understanding deepens, and you pivot based on feedback and learning.

Post its creation, the Business Model Canvas is a living document that should be frequently revisited and refined. Given the fluid nature of market dynamics and venture progression, it's critical to keep iterating on the canvas details. This iterative process ensures your business model remains robust, relevant, and adaptable—aiding in successfully navigating the startup journey.

Now, armed with a clear understanding of your business model, we can go deeper into its core building blocks. Each piece should fit together to construct a coherent, compelling narrative that not only resonates with your target audience but drives your startup's trajectory to a viable business.

The GTM Strategy Puzzle

Your Go-To-Market strategy is akin to a multifaceted jigsaw puzzle. At its core are the foundational pieces: knowledge of the market, insight into the competition, understanding of your customers, and clarity around what value you bring to the table. Once the core components are in place and you have clarified these strategic components, you turn your focus to the execution phase, which requires disciplined sales and marketing activities. The key as you enter that stage is to ensure a consistent narrative that threads through all channels of communication. And the final part of the puzzle involves the crucial selection of metrics (calibrated to fit the venture's lifestyle stage) to measure, monitor, and enhance your strategy's effectiveness, allowing you to iterate and adapt when necessary.

I firmly hold the view that a GTM strategy quintessentially should revolve around the customer. The customer is the north star of the business—without whom no business is viable. What is more, we need to take both an outside-in and inside-out perspective. The first (outside-in) involves looking at it from the customer experience vantage point while the other (inside-out) considers the integration of business functions (sales, marketing, operations). At its core, however, it is about any aspect of our strategy that can improve (or impair) the likelihood of customer purchase and renewal—the focal point of our efforts.

I cannot emphasize enough the critical importance of dedicating sufficient time and resources to meticulously crafting a GTM strategy **before** diving into execution. It's a common pitfall for founders to hastily sketch out a rudimentary strategy in their eagerness to move to the execution phase. This rush often stems from a misplaced optimism (bordering on certainty) that their product is so exceptional that it will naturally captivate the market.

This overconfidence is further fueled by the allure of "getting things done," the satisfaction derived from ticking off boxes on to-do lists. However, this premature confidence often deflates when the anticipated results fail to materialize, so it's imperative to make well-considered strategic choices, plan meticulously, and only then proceed to execution.

(FIGURE 21: GTM STRATEGY)

Understanding this cautionary tale serves as a segue into recognizing the delicate balance between value creation and value capture that underpins any successful GTM strategy. Value creation revolves around solving tangible problems for customers, a concept that aligns closely with Dan Olsen's "problem space" framework. Conversely, value capture is about converting a portion of the value created into tangible profit. This can be achieved through various means such as pricing strategies, licensing agreements, subscription models, or other revenue-generating avenues.

In essence, crafting a robust GTM strategy requires a laser focus on the WHAT, WHO, WHERE, HOW, and WHY of your business. As I've already argued, this process is not just about making choices; it's equally about consciously deciding what avenues not to explore. This dual focus ensures that your strategy is both comprehensive and targeted, setting the stage for successful execution.

Your understanding of the customers' problems and the solutions you offer will guide your choice of distribution channels and pricing strategy. One key decision is whether to prioritize operational excellence, product leadership, or customer intimacy, a framework defined in *The Discipline of Market Leaders*, although as we've already argued, academic startups tend to overwhelmingly focus (at least initially) on their technological core, the *product*.

Setting Sail on Your GTM Voyage

Launching a product is like setting off on a treasure hunt. Your map? Market knowledge. Survey the landscape, spot potential treasures, and decide where to dig.

Think of yourself as a detective when creating a product that will be marketed in the real world. Explore in great detail your customer's needs and motivations. What troubles them? What do they want? Group them by needs, habits, and whatever other characteristic you feel is pertinent for a given context. By understanding these segments, you can shape your product to snugly fit into their lives.

Every product needs its own story, a reason it exists. This is your value proposition. It's a pledge that says, "This is how I'll improve your life." This story should strike a chord with your audience and guide your marketing and sales. It needs to be compelling, memorable, and easy to understand.

Building and maintaining customer relationships is so fundamental that it borders on cliche. But it's not just about a one-time sale. Engage with your customers, assist them, reward their loyalty, and heed their feedback. This isn't just courtesy; it's smart business. A satisfied customer comes back. Your relationship approach should harmonize with your product's narrative and help further build and scale your business. As Peter Drucker famously quipped, "there is only one purpose of a business: to create a customer."

Once you have a product and its compelling narrative, it's essential to broadcast your message with consistency, clarity, and vigor. Choose channels that deeply resonate with your target audience. Picture it as a grand concert: marketing lays the foundation, sales draw in the audience, and customer support delivers an encore performance. When each component synergizes perfectly, the concert becomes memorable.

Behind every exceptional product lies a meticulously orchestrated operation. This encompasses finances, logistics, and astute pricing strategies. Indeed, you need to be acutely aware of your venture's financial dynamics—which is not just about tracking numbers, but also deciphering the narrative they weave regarding your business's vitality, potential for expansion, and avenues for refinement. By all means, examine the specifics of your inflows and outflows, and dissect the complexities of your cost structures. This financial insight is the backbone of efficient operations. When operations are streamlined based on a clear financial understanding, they not only ensure consistent delivery but also fortify brand trust and engender loyalty.

As for your product's price, it's more than just a number; it's a declaration of its worth. It should not only cover costs but also ensure profitability. Remember, price often serves as a proxy for value. Contrary to traditional economic theories that painted us as purely rational actors, modern understanding recognizes that our purchasing decisions are influenced by emotions, perceptions, and biases. The price, therefore, becomes a psychological cue, signaling the product's value and quality in the marketplace.

Finally, as you navigate your business operations, you need a system to monitor performance, learn, and adjust when necessary. Keep tabs on sales, feedback, and market shifts. This is about flexibility, not micromanagement. Adapt and ensure your product stays relevant and remember that every journey has its challenges. If things veer off course, pivot. It's about how you adapt and flourish.

There are several metrics to gauge your GTM strategy's performance. While these depend on your startup's phase, some universal metrics include:

- **Leads:** Count of potential customers from marketing and sales.

- **Conversion rate:** Percentage of leads becoming customers.

- **Customer lifetime value:** Average spend of a customer over time.

- **ROI:** Profit from your GTM strategy relative to its cost.

Based on these metrics, be ready to pivot if things aren't panning out. However, some companies hesitate to change due to the sunk cost fallacy. They dwell on their past investments and efforts, using them as a reason to not let go. They are under the illusion that costs already incurred are still relevant to our current and future decisions, when in fact they are not. That's why they are called "sunk costs."

Indeed, once we have made an investment, we cannot get the money back, so it is irrelevant to our future decision calculus. The only thing that matters is whether or not the investment is still a good one. If not, we need to cut our losses and move on.

The sunk cost fallacy is deeply rooted in our intrinsic aversion to loss, a cognitive bias that often subtly influences our decisions. This bias arises from a psychological imbalance or asymmetry between loss and reward, such that the sting of a loss often resonates more deeply than the joy of a comparable gain—leading to choices that are suboptimal or, sometimes, downright irrational.

So, let's now move to our case study, Palantir. Its journey presents a real-world testament to the impact of a well-crafted business model combined with a robust GTM strategy.

CASE STUDY: PALANTIR

Palantir Technologies is a software company that develops data analysis platforms for the government and commercial sectors. Founded in 2003 by a group of Stanford University alumni including Peter Thiel and Alex Karp, the company's initial focus was on anti-fraud analysis. However, the company quickly pivoted to developing advanced data analysis platforms that could help organizations make better decisions by bridging human intuition with machine-powered analytical capabilities.

(FIGURE 22: PALANTIR)

The venture's GTM strategy has been one of its key strengths. It has focused on a niche yet vital customer base: the U.S. government, specifically intelligence agencies and defense departments. The venture's flagship product, Palantir Gotham, was designed to extract complex patterns from vast, diverse data sources—a capability that gained significant traction in the post-9/11 context, where comprehensive data analysis was pivotal in tackling complex and sensitive security challenges.

Palantir's GTM strategy has been characterized by its focus on customer intimacy. The company has built deep relationships with its customers, understanding their specific needs and challenges. This has allowed Palantir to tailor its products and services to meet the unique requirements of each customer.

Palantir has also been innovative in its GTM strategy. The company has been willing to experiment with new marketing and sales channels. For example, Palantir has used social media to reach out to potential customers and build relationships. The company has also used its products to demonstrate its value to customers, rather than simply relying on traditional sales pitches.

As Palantir matured, it began to broaden its target market. The company now has customers in the financial services, healthcare, and energy sectors. Palantir's GTM strategy for these new markets has been similar to its approach in the government sector: focus on customer intimacy and innovation.

Palantir's GTM strategy has been a key factor in the company's success. The company has grown rapidly and become a leading provider of data analysis platforms. Palantir's GTM strategy is a model for other companies that are looking to succeed in the data-driven economy.

Highlights: Palantir's GTM strategy has focused on customer intimacy. It has been innovative in its GTM strategy, using social media and its products to reach out to potential customers, and has done this very effectively.

CHAPTER 9:
Essential Tools & Analytical Frameworks

Startups, with their limited resources, face steep challenges in their quest for market penetration. A meticulously crafted GTM strategy can offer a clear roadmap to navigate what are crowded and often highly competitive marketplaces. Integral to this strategy is the arsenal of tools and solutions tailored for data gathering and analysis, which were once exclusive to large corporations.

In the preceding chapter, we discussed the significance of a GTM strategy and how to craft one as the basis for methodical and meticulous execution. In this chapter, we turn our attention to the specific tools and solutions that can help startups to actualize their strategic vision, based on evidence rather than mere intuition or wishful thinking.

Today's digital technology offers startups a plethora of affordable tools, spanning areas from marketing and sales to customer service and operations. These tools not only enhance reach and efficiency but also level the playing field, allowing new ventures to compete with more established corporate giants.

A pivotal asset for startups is marketing insights. Historically, such insights were the domain of large corporations with deep pockets, investing in premium marketing analytics and support from an array of high-powered research or specialized consulting firms. However, the rise of big data analytics has democratized access, enabling startups to harness critical insights without the hefty price tag that comes with engaging consultants or large research firms.

This newfound accessibility to marketing data empowers startups to make informed decisions, refine their marketing mix, and monitor outcomes with precision. By judiciously choosing and deploying these tools, startups can carve a niche, scale effectively, and maintain their competitiveness.

Toolkits for Marketing Insights

In this chapter, we explore the diverse range of decision-support tools, spanning from market research techniques to problem-framing methodologies. For quick reference, a comprehensive list of these tools is available in Appendix C.

While the specific tools and solutions you choose will be tailored to your startup's unique GTM strategy, certain core areas hold universal significance for startups:

Social Intelligence

In our interconnected digital era, understanding the intricate web of conversations about products and services is essential—and provides hereto untapped sources of customer insight. By sifting through the ever-expanding digital dialogues, from tweets and public feedback to more private interactions like chat messages, companies can discover new opportunities, anticipate potential challenges, and pinpoint areas for improvement.

As McKinsey's 2020 report highlights, data-driven organizations are 23% more likely to achieve above-average profitability. The rise of social listening and digital research tools can be traced back to an array of interconnected technological breakthroughs. While the widespread adoption of the internet and advancements in computing power set the stage, the real game-changer has been the innovations in artificial intelligence (AI) and deep learning. These cutting-edge technologies have not only accelerated data analysis but have also endowed it with unparalleled depth and precision.

Indeed, harnessing the vast reservoirs of online data can provide businesses with a competitive advantage. With over 95% of data being unstructured, many companies find themselves overwhelmed, unable to unlock its inherent value. But with the emergence of affordable AI-driven platforms, businesses can now dissect audience demographics, monitor brand perceptions, assess campaigns, and identify emerging market trends.

This technological evolution has spawned numerous ventures in the marketing insights domain, including notable names like Crimson Hexagon, Brandwatch, and Sysomos. Among these pioneers is DMR, where I hold the position of Advisory Board Chair. Recognizing the transformative potential of digital capabilities early on, DMR's leadership pivoted from a primarily professional service orientation to a technology-centric model where speed, accuracy, and multi-lingual capabilities were the core propositions. They went about building an offering where advanced digital platforms, powered by machine learning, are complemented by a robust professional services team to provide customer decision support.

DMR's flagship platform, Listening 247, adeptly employs AI to traverse the vast landscape of social media data, converting it into actionable insights that echo public sentiment, be it in Tagalog, Japanese, or Mandarin. The platform stands on two foundational pillars:

- **Customer Insights**: This facet offers a deep dive into customer viewpoints. By meticulously analyzing social media interactions, call center dialogues, and survey feedback, businesses can segment their audience, crafting strategies to elevate customer satisfaction.

- **Competition Insights**: This dimension emphasizes vigilant monitoring of competitors' digital footprints. By staying attuned to competitors' online maneuvers, startups can strategize proactively and pinpoint untapped market opportunities.

For example, DMR's platform was used by a leading global firm to reshape its customer experience strategy. By analyzing public posts in social media, blogs, and forums for unsolicited conversations around their brand and competitors, the firm was able to gauge the level of customer engagement, identify areas where their brand excelled, and pinpoint potential pain points or areas for improvement through optimizing the customer journey and experience. This information was then used to improve the firm's customer service processes, resulting in a significant improvement in customer engagement.

The platform also enables businesses to monitor their competitors' digital footprints and current marketing mix activities. This information can be used to identify new market opportunities, stay ahead of the competition, and avoid costly mistakes.

Overall, social intelligence is a powerful tool that can help businesses to make better decisions, improve their performance, and stay ahead of the competition.

Market Research: Expanding Capabilities

Even with the rise of increasingly sophisticated and powerful social listening tools, startups of all sizes still need to conduct market research. While social intelligence is a hugely valuable tool, it cannot provide all the information that startups need. For example, social intelligence can tell you what people are saying about your product or service, but you may still need to probe why they are saying it. To get this information, startups need to reach out to customers, ask questions, and use more traditional investigative methods.

This information can be used to develop products and services that meet customer needs, identify potential risks, and avoid costly mistakes. For example, a startup that is developing a new mobile app could use market research to understand the demographics of potential users, their needs and preferences, their willingness to pay for the app, and a range of "why" questions that we may not be able to elicit answers to via social listening.

So, in today's digital era, the availability and advancement of online tools have fundamentally reshaped market research methodologies. What used to be a capability that could be tapped into by large corporates is now available to smaller companies. Indeed, now startups can gather richer insights with more agility, at a fraction of what it used to cost. This democratization of research not only empowers them with essential data but may even provide a competitive edge.

Market Research Tools:

The market research industry is vast, with a spectrum of vendors from global giants like Ipsos and Kantar TNS to regional specialists. My own firm, MASMI Research Group, has carved out a niche by offering bespoke marketing insights tailored for Central/Eastern Europe and the Middle East. Our unique positioning combines cutting-edge research tools with a deep understanding of local nuances, combined with extensive sectoral expertise through hundreds of research projects.

Quantitative Research: Going Digital

In the past, startups heavily relied on face-to-face surveys and telephonic interviews. The advent of digital technologies has pivoted these interactions to online platforms, enabling access to wider audiences quickly and conveniently. This shift not only minimizes logistical challenges but also enhances the precision of data and boosts respondent participation.

The digital realm, spanning from social media to specialized survey websites, has opened direct communication channels to a variety of audiences. These platforms make it seamless for startups to gather feedback, assess product-market fit, and foster early-stage customer engagement, laying the foundation for long-term loyalty.

Qualitative Research: The Digital Evolution

The rise of digital technology has had a profound impact on qualitative research. Traditional methods, such as focus groups and in-depth interviews, have been adapted for the online environment, making it possible to reach a wider range of participants and collect richer data.

One of the most significant changes has been the move from physical to virtual settings. Focus groups and interviews can now be conducted online using video conferencing software, which allows participants to interact with each other and the moderator in real time. This has several advantages, including:

- Overcoming geographical barriers: Participants can join from anywhere in the world, which can be especially beneficial for businesses or organizations with a global reach.

- Attracting a richer mix of participants: Online research can reach a wider range of people, including those who are unable or unwilling to travel to a physical location.

- Reducing costs: Conducting research online can be more cost-effective than traditional methods, as there is no need to rent a facility or pay for travel expenses.

Leveraging Online Communities

In addition to virtual focus groups and interviews, qualitative researchers are also leveraging digital communities to gather insights. These communities can be dedicated to specific interests, brands, or demographics, and they provide a platform for participants to share their thoughts and experiences in a natural and unscripted way.

Digital communities offer several advantages for qualitative research, including:

- Instantaneous feedback: Researchers can get feedback from participants in real time, which can help them to refine their questions and explore new ideas.

- Restoring social dynamics: Digital communities can help to restore the interactive social dynamics that are often lost in traditional research. This can lead to richer and more nuanced insights.

- Facilitating peer interactions: Digital communities can facilitate peer interactions, which can produce organic, spontaneous insights that would not be possible in a traditional setting.

Evolving Trends in Market Research

The digital age has revolutionized market research, leading to innovative methodologies that promise deeper insights and higher accuracy. Neuromarketing, for instance, taps into physiological and neural responses to product stimuli, offering a window into the subconscious preferences of consumers. By measuring brain activity during interactions with advertisements or product packaging, businesses can fine-tune their marketing strategies for maximum impact.

Virtual reality (VR) is another frontier in market research. By creating immersive environments, VR allows researchers to observe how consumers interact with products in simulated settings. This can be invaluable for product testing, customer experience enhancement, and feedback collection before a product's market launch.

Yet, as with all technological advancements, there are ethical considerations so we must tread carefully. Neuromarketing, with its deep dive into the human psyche, raises questions about privacy and the potential for misuse. Similarly, VR's immersive experiences could be used unethically, playing on consumers' fears or emotions. It's crucial for market researchers to navigate these tools with integrity, ensuring that participants' rights and well-being are always prioritized.

Secondary Research in the Digital Age

The internet has democratized access to information, transforming secondary research. Startups can now delve into a plethora of resources, from academic studies to competitors' disclosures. But the true revolution lies in AI-powered analytics. These tools can sift through vast data sets, extracting patterns and insights that can shape a startup's direction. Such capabilities, once exclusive to large corporations, are now within reach for startups, leveling the playing field.

Experimental Research and the AI Revolution

Experimental research too has been redefined by digital advancements. Rapid prototyping, facilitated by cloud platforms, allows for swift product iterations. The MVP approach, essential for many startups, benefits from real-time feedback loops. Moreover, A/B testing, a staple in digital marketing, has been supercharged by AI, enabling more accurate predictions and refinements.

As I've already argued, ethical considerations, especially around data privacy and algorithmic biases, are very real. As startups harness AI and vast data sets, they must ensure fairness, transparency, and respect for individual rights. In this evolving context, ethical diligence isn't just a moral imperative—it's a business necessity.

Evaluating Intellectual Property (IP)

For startups, intellectual property is both a shield and a sword. It safeguards innovations and can be a significant draw for investors. However, navigating the IP landscape requires discernment. Tools like patent search engines, copyright and trademark registrations, and trade secret protections are invaluable. But beyond tools, startups benefit from expert guidance. IP professionals, be they lawyers or consultants, can demystify the complexities of IP, ensuring startups not only protect their innovations but also leverage them for growth. As startups journey through the IP maze, proactive measures, informed strategies, and expert counsel are their best allies.

Some of the most common tools for evaluating IP include:

- **Patent search engines**: These tools can be used to search for patents that have been granted in a particular country or region. This can help startups to identify potential competitors and to assess the strength of their own IP.

- **Copyright registration**: Copyright registration can help to protect original works of authorship, such as books, articles, music, and software. This can help startups to prevent others from copying or distributing their work without permission.

- **Trademark registration**: Trademark registration can help to protect words, phrases, symbols, and designs that are used to identify a particular product or service. This can help startups to prevent others from using their trademarks to confuse consumers.

- **Trade secret protection**: Trade secret protection can help to protect confidential information, such as formulas, recipes, and business processes. This can help startups to prevent others from stealing their trade secrets and using them to gain a competitive advantage.

In addition to these tools, there are a number of other resources available to startups for evaluating IP, but one needs to reach out to specialists with the requisite skills such as IP lawyers or IP consultants.

Finally, when it comes to IP protection it is advisable to be highly proactive. Don't wait until someone infringes on your IP to take action. Start protecting your IP early on.

Insights to Action: Frameworks & Tools

After exploring a diverse range of business analytic tools, we have established a foundational understanding of the tools startups can employ to deeply comprehend their market and customers, and evaluate and protect their IP. These tools are the bedrock upon which academic startups can base their strategic decisions and pivot if necessary.

However, as startups navigate their journey, they will often need to draw on conceptual frameworks or specific techniques that are designed for specific challenges. These might overlap with the foundational tools but may sometimes require a focused and bespoke approach.

Strategic Analysis: Charting the Course

In the realm of startups, strategic analysis is akin to a captain charting a course through uncharted waters. Tools like McKinsey's MECE help us logically group information into elements that are "mutually exclusive" (ME) and "collectively exhaustive" (CE). It provides a process whereby information—ideas, topics, issues, solutions—is arranged in the appropriate "bucket" with no overlap with other "buckets" while ensuring that the totality of an issue is captured.

Then we have SWOT Analysis, a popular quadrant-based tool, that prompts startups to introspectively assess their strengths and weaknesses (internal factors) while also scanning the horizon for opportunities and threats (external factors).

PESTEL Analysis, meanwhile, broadens the lens, examining macro-environmental factors that might influence a startup's journey. The fusion of these traditional tools with AI's predictive modeling capabilities supercharges their efficacy. For instance, AI-enhanced SWOT analysis can forecast the impact of leveraging a particular strength on market dynamics.

Goal Setting: The North Star

Every startup's journey needs direction. SMART goals, which are *specific, measurable, achievable, relevant,* and *time-bound*, act as detailed navigational charts to enable us to track actions and monitor progress, typically withing a well-defined time horizon.

Objectives and Key results (OKRs) is a somewhat different goal-setting framework that is often used in software development projects. It consists of two parts: objectives, which are qualitative statements of what you want to achieve, and key results, which are quantitative measures of progress towards the objectives. OKRs are often used for long-term goals and because of their flexibility, they work particularly well with so-called "agile" approaches (that prioritize cross-functional collaboration and continuous improvement).

These two frameworks, often used in combination, ensure that every step, whether it's a minor adjustment or a major leap, aligns with the startup's overarching vision and more detailed goals.

Pricing: Striking the Right Balance

Pricing is a delicate balancing act. The startup needs to set a price that is high enough to generate a profit, but not so high that it drives away customers. There are three main pricing strategies: cost-plus pricing, value-based pricing, and competitive pricing. Cost-plus pricing is the simplest approach, but it may not be the most profitable. Value-based pricing sets the price based on the perceived value of the product or service. Competitive pricing sets the price based on the prices of other similar products or services.

Marketing and Sales: Amplifying the Message

In the startup ecosystem, communication tools are paramount. Platforms like Salesforce transcend mere automation, offering insights into sales trends and customer behaviors. Similarly, Mailchimp and its ilk have transformed email campaigns, while tools like Hootsuite and Buffer orchestrate a brand's social media symphony. These tools are not just about broadcasting a message; they're about engaging in a dialogue with the audience and adapting based on their feedback.

Performance Tracking: The Pulse Check

A startup's journey is dynamic, demanding regular pulse checks. While tools like Google Analytics offer insights into digital interactions, AI-enhanced platforms delve deeper, predicting future trends. Beyond mere website analytics, these tools gauge brand awareness, customer engagement, and other vital metrics, offering a holistic view of a startup's health. The key is to set clear objectives, choose the right tools, and continuously refine strategies based on data-driven insights.

Of course, no set of tools can guarantee success. Ultimately, it is the startup's vision, adaptability, and relentless pursuit of excellence that will determine its fate. But by using the right tools and frameworks, and arming themselves with evidence, startups can give themselves a better chance of achieving their goals.

Now let's conclude the chapter with our case study on Slack that showcases its pivoting to fill a communications gap.

CASE STUDY: SLACK

Slack, today's widely used workplace communication platform, began as an internal tool during a completely different project. Its journey from an incidental tool to a market leader showcases the power of strategic analysis and the importance of adaptability.

While working on a gaming project, Stewart Butterfield and his team stumbled upon a challenge: the need for centralized communication. Recognizing the broader potential of their internal communication tool, they decided to pivot, turning this tool into what we now know as Slack.

(FIGURE 23: SLACK)

Their decision to pivot was not impulsive. Market research revealed a glaring gap: businesses lacked an efficient, unified communication platform. With this knowledge, they crafted a Minimum Viable Product (MVP)—a basic version of Slack. But the journey didn't stop there. Embracing the Lean Startup methodology, they continuously refined Slack based on feedback from its early users.

Butterfield's team spared no effort to truly understand their potential users. They envisioned their ideal customers as tech-savvy businesses, weary of disjointed communication tools. By mapping out the customer journey, from the first interaction to becoming loyal users, they tailored their platform's features and user experience, emphasizing seamless onboarding and compatibility with other tools.

Slack's unique chat interface and its core features were safeguarded through intellectual property rights, ensuring its innovative approach remained highly competitive. Using a variety of analytical and strategic tools like PESTEL to gauge external market dynamics and the competitive environment, the team honed the company's unique value proposition in the crowded tech market.

Every strategy at Slack was tied to clear, measurable objectives. These were prioritized, and progress was tracked continuously. Their pricing strategy, built on a freemium model, aimed to first attract a broad user base and then offer premium features, aligning with a value-based pricing approach.

Slack's marketing campaigns, known for their wit and relatability, resonated with audiences. Word-of-mouth referrals further amplified their reach. To ensure their marketing efforts bore fruit, they employed analytics tools, continuously learning and iterating based on the insights gathered.

Highlights: Slack's transformation from an incidental tool during a gaming project to a leading workplace communication platform showcases strategic adaptability. Recognizing a market need for unified business communication, the team pivoted, continuously refining Slack based on user feedback. Their deep understanding of tech-savvy businesses, combined with strategic analytical tools, helped carve a unique market position. With clear, measurable objectives and a freemium pricing model, the company's witty marketing campaigns and data-driven strategies propelled its growth and market resonance.

CHAPTER 10:
Unraveling the Threads of Market Opportunity

Entrepreneurship is an expedition into the unknown, a journey through uncharted territories. A robust understanding of the market serves as your compass, guiding your venture through complexities and leading it towards opportunities. Identifying key market dynamics, drivers, and boundaries isn't just about understanding the current state of play. It's about predicting where your industry might head, what trends may emerge, and which problems your startup is poised to solve. It's a blend of science and art, of analytical rigor and creative foresight.

Market analysis, which might seem straightforward initially, often turns out to be more intricate and challenging. In this chapter, we examine the art and science of market analysis and both the macro and micro levels. Here, we provide a roadmap that helps unravel the complexities of the market landscape and efficiently position your academic startup. We will incorporate the lessons learned from market research methodologies and social listening tools discussed in the previous chapter. These approaches, employed at both macro (industry trends) and micro (specific offerings) levels, can be critical in identifying and exploiting market opportunities.

Whether it's gleaning insights from big-picture industry trends or fine-tuning your service offerings based on feedback and sentiment analysis, each layer of market understanding adds another thread to the tapestry of your market opportunity. Your objective is to weave these threads together, creating a vivid picture of where you fit in the marketplace, who your customers are, and how you can best serve them. So let's begin this journey of unraveling the threads of market opportunity and weaving them into a strategic narrative for your venture.

What is important to underscore is that understanding the market is a multi-layered exercise. You don't just do it once and move on. Let's start with the macro-level.

Macro-Level Analysis: Industry Trends

Understanding the market is not a one-dimensional task; it's a multi-layered endeavor that demands both breadth and depth. On the macro level, casting a wide net to capture the larger currents of industry trends, global shifts, and broad societal changes becomes indispensable.

Here, tools like Porter's Five Forces and PESTEL analysis lay down the foundation. Yet, to truly harness the granularity and nuance within this vast landscape, insights from established firms like Gartner and Frost & Sullivan play a crucial role.

Gartner, for instance, offers insights that can help identify significant technological trends. Their Hype Cycles, charting the evolution of technological innovations from inception to mainstream adoption, allow startups to position themselves at the cusp of disruptions or opportunities. More specifically, the report provides a unique representation of the maturity, adoption, and social application of specific technologies. Visualized as a graph, it illustrates five distinct phases of a technology's life cycle: the "Innovation Trigger," where a new technology is conceptualized; the "Peak of Inflated Expectations," marked by a surge of enthusiasm and rapid adoption; the "Trough of Disillusionment," a period of skepticism and waning interest following unmet expectations; the "Slope of Enlightenment," where the technology's true value begins to crystallize and practical applications emerge; and finally, the "Plateau of Productivity," where the technology becomes widely adopted and its benefits are well-understood. For startups and businesses, the Hype Cycle offers invaluable insights into the potential risks and rewards of investing in emerging technologies. By understanding where a technology sits on the cycle, firms can make informed decisions about when to adopt, invest, or develop a particular innovation.

As we sift through the economic and technological segments of a PESTEL analysis, reports from Frost & Sullivan act as anchors, grounding our understanding in empirical, evidence-based insights. For example, to better understand the economic factors, Frost & Sullivan offers comprehensive market forecasts, detailing growth opportunities and elucidating key economic drivers and restraints. Their reports often cover supply chain dynamics, mapping out potential choke points or areas of vulnerability that might impact the industry's profitability. They might also provide an analysis of various economic scenarios—ranging from baseline to bullish or bearish outlooks—that can help businesses prepare for different economic climates and pivot their strategies accordingly.

On the technological front, Frost & Sullivan's reports can be very helpful in understanding emerging tech trends and their potential market impact. They assess the technological readiness of various innovations, highlighting those that are poised to disrupt existing market dynamics. Moreover, these reports often contain in-depth technology benchmarks, comparing different innovations based on factors such as efficiency, scalability, and integration capabilities. They might also provide insights into potential partnerships or acquisition targets in the tech space, spotlighting companies that are leading the charge in R&D and innovation.

In essence, leveraging such insights allows businesses to tap into a rich repository of data, ensuring that their PESTEL analysis is both robust and informed by the latest industry developments.

Recognizing the value in these mosaic pieces and fitting them into a coherent big picture is essential. With the combination of robust analytical tools and industry-leading insights, startups gain a compass to navigate their macro environment with precision.

Diving into Macro Analytical Tools

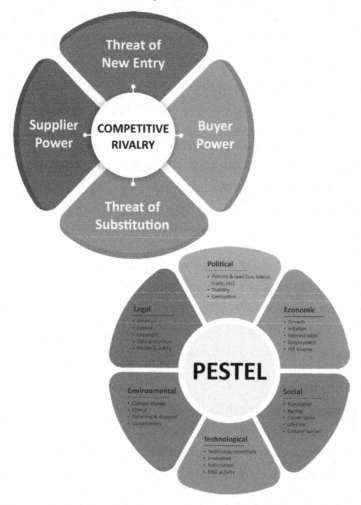

(FIGURES 24.1 AND 24.2: THE FIVE FORCES & PESTEL MODELS)

The Five Forces Framework, developed by Michael Porter, offers a holistic lens to comprehend an industry's inherent dynamics and the competitive forces that shape it. It dissects the landscape into:

1. **Competitive Rivalry:** Representing the competitive intensity among existing industry players.

2. **Threat of New Entrants:** Assessing the ease with which new competitors can carve their niche in the industry.

3. **Threat of Substitutes:** Evaluating the potential of customers transitioning to alternative solutions.

4. **Bargaining Power of Suppliers:** Gauging the control suppliers wield over pricing and supply dynamics.

5. **Bargaining Power of Buyers:** Measuring the influence customers have in steering price negotiations and product demand.

PESTEL analysis, in contrast, probes the external macro-environmental forces that could sway an organization's trajectory. Represented by the acronym denoting Political, Economic, Social, Technological, Environmental, and Legal factors, PESTEL provides startups with a panoramic view of potential opportunities and threats in the larger context.

For instance, an academic startup pioneering in green energy solutions would be well-advised to employ both these strategic tools. Through the Five Forces, they can gauge their position in the green energy ecosystem, while PESTEL empowers them to understand the broader socio-political, economic, and technological realms they operate within.

To contextualize with our green energy startup: if they earmark utility companies aspiring to diminish their carbon footprint as their primary customer segment, a report from Frost & Sullivan could unveil insights about the size and growth potential of this segment, key industry players, pricing stratagems, and forecasted trends. Armed with this knowledge, the startup can sharpen its value proposition.

At the heart of the startup's value proposition are the cost savings and environmental advantages of their technology promises. By discerning the decision-making criteria and challenges of utility companies, the startup can tailor its offerings more precisely, ensuring they resonate with customers and offer a competitive edge.

In today's globalized markets, where startups frequently target international niches, the importance of local knowledge is paramount. Market research institutions, with their local resources, equip startups with foundational insights, but it's the startup's on-ground interactions with potential customers and partners that solidify their understanding. This balance between global strategies and local nuances is what paves the way for success.

To bolster these assessments, sentiment analysis offers further insights:

- **Industry Trends:** Social media platforms brim with discourses on evolving industry patterns. Through social listening tools, startups can tune into the collective consciousness, extracting invaluable insights from industry frontrunners and the wider consumer base.

- **Competitive Analysis:** Tracking competitors becomes more dynamic with sentiment analysis. Startups can gauge the efficacy of competitors' marketing maneuvers and customer engagement, refining their own strategies based on public sentiment.

- **Market Sentiment:** Especially in turbulent economic climates, sentiment analysis becomes a barometer of consumer sentiments, hopes, and anxieties.

With this macro perspective in hand, our attention shifts to the micro realm, where firm-specific intricacies come into sharper focus.

Micro-Level Analysis

When we get into micro-level market analysis, we focus on the specific elements impacting our venture, from discerning customer needs and pricing trends to understanding the competitive landscape. Navigating this intricate terrain necessitates dependable insights. Traditional market research giants undeniably offer unparalleled depth, but their costs might deter early-stage ventures. However, astute investments in such insights, combined with more affordable alternatives like sentiment analysis on social media, can yield a well-rounded understanding of the market.

In addition to general market research firms, there are also a number of resources available that technology startups can tap into for market insights specific to their industry or niche. These include:

- Technology research firms like Gartner, Forrester, IDC that provide detailed analysis on technology markets.

- Industry associations and non-profits that produce market reports. For example, the Consumer Technology Association for consumer tech.

- Open data platforms like data.gov that provide public access to government and other data sets.

- Pitchbook and Crunchbase for private company data to analyze competitors.

- Networking events and industry conferences to connect with customers, partners, experts.

- Customer discovery interviews and focus groups for direct customer feedback.

Armed with these micro-level insights, startups can complement their big-picture perspective, gaining an intimate understanding of their particular market landscape. This multifaceted comprehension empowers them to craft sharply focused value propositions, choose effective market entry strategies, and continually refine their approach based on real-world signals.

Refining Your Market Understanding

Market analysis isn't a static endeavor but an evolving, iterative process. Markets pulse and breathe, shaped by a medley of factors—consumer behavior, technological leaps, economic oscillations, political winds, and socio-cultural tides. A vigilant eye on these evolving patterns isn't just advantageous; it's imperative.

While startups, especially those juggling tight purse strings, might not have the luxury of tapping into bespoke market research or market tracking services as provided by stalwarts like Ipsos or Kantar, the digital age presents them with an array of cost-effective alternatives. Continuous market understanding isn't merely an academic exercise; it's the lifeblood of businesses aiming to disrupt and differentiate.

A quintessential tool in the cost-effective arsenal is social listening and sentiment analysis. These tools, with their real-time pulse on customer moods and market shifts, become invaluable navigational aids. By distilling the emotions behind the cacophony of social media voices, startups can anticipate shifts in market preferences, recalibrating their strategies in stride.

But the rhythm of refining market understanding doesn't end there. It calls for a recurring dance of revisiting and revamping your Ideal Customer Profile (ICP)—a dance informed by the echoes of customer feedback and the rhythm of data-driven insights. It's about having your ear to the ground, detecting tremors of industry changes, and scouting the horizon for potential opportunities or looming threats. Adaptability isn't just a buzzword. In a volatile market landscape—epitomized by phenomena like the COVID-19 pandemic—it's a survival trait.

This refining journey could employ an array of tools: accessible yet potent analytics platforms, scheduled rendezvous with customers for feedback, or self-curated mechanisms to monitor the ebb and flow of market trends and competitor maneuvers. Even when operating on a shoestring budget, ensuring that your strategy is robustly data-centric, agile, and tenacious is entirely feasible. The digital realm, resplendent with resources like affordable sentiment analysis tools, AI powerhouses like ChatGPT, and the pulse of industry updates via professional networks, becomes the compass guiding startups through uncharted waters.

Augmented with social listening tools, and armed with industry reports, you can attain a solid understanding of the consumer sentiment surrounding your brand, your competitors, and the industry at large. This real-time feedback enables prompt adaptation to changing market dynamics and evolving consumer preferences.

Frost & Sullivan's growth-centric model is crafted to support clients through all five phases of the growth cycle:

1. Developing a pipeline of growth opportunities

2. Evaluating and prioritizing those opportunities

3. Formulating and executing go-to-market strategies

4. Monitoring and refining strategies

5. Cultivating the subsequent pipeline of growth opportunities

Such services can empower startups with a good understanding of their market, helping them with decision-making and strategy development during the pivotal go-to-market phase.

Attuned to Local Contexts

In today's globalized markets, where startups frequently target international niches, the importance of local knowledge is paramount. Market research institutions, with their local resources, equip startups with foundational insights, but it's the startup's on-ground interactions with potential customers and partners that solidify their understanding. This balance between global strategies and local nuances is what paves the way for success.

Local knowledge is not merely about cultural insights; it encompasses market idiosyncrasies, regulatory blueprints, consumer behavior, and competition. Harnessing this knowledge can furnish startups with a strategic advantage, unveiling untapped market opportunities.

For academic startups, this local knowledge cannot be overstated. It entails grasping not just consumer insights but also the multifaceted dynamics of industries where their pioneering technologies might find application.

As we conclude this chapter, it is important to emphasize that combining marketing research and social listening can give startups a deeper and more nuanced understanding of their market, enabling them to navigate their market journeys with greater precision and insight.

Let's now turn to our case study on SolarCity.

CASE STUDY: SOLARCITY

SolarCity, a brainchild of brothers Lyndon and Peter Rive and supported by their cousin Elon Musk, is a testament to the power of discerning market opportunities and addressing them effectively. It capitalized on a pivotal moment when the world was increasingly recognizing the need for renewable energy. Therefore, the untapped potential of solar power was ripe for exploration. It was the right time, in a game where timing is often the most critical factor for success.

(FIGURE 25: SOLARCITY)

By way of background, in the early 2000s, the solar energy market was still in its infancy. Consumers were increasingly interested in solar power, but the high upfront costs, installation complexities, and maintenance responsibilities were formidable obstacles.

SolarCity recognized this growing demand and the barriers that were preventing consumers from adopting solar power. The company's founders, Lyndon and Peter Rive, saw an opportunity to disrupt the market and make solar power more accessible and affordable.

Developing a Disruptive Business Model

SolarCity's business model was designed to address the key barriers to solar adoption. The company offered to lease and install solar panels for customers, eliminating the need for a large upfront investment. SolarCity also handled all maintenance and repairs, giving customers peace of mind.

In addition, SolarCity offered its electricity at a lower rate than traditional utilities. This made solar power more affordable than ever before and helped to reduce customers' energy bills.

Expanding to Meet Demand

SolarCity's business model proved successful, and the company quickly expanded its reach across the United States. As it expanded, SolarCity adapted its approach to each market to meet local demand and regulations. For example, in California, SolarCity partnered with the state government to offer solar leases to low-income households.

SolarCity's success caught the attention of Tesla, Inc., which acquired the company in 2016. Tesla's acquisition helped to further legitimize solar power and accelerate its adoption.

Impact on the Solar Energy Market

SolarCity played a significant role in popularizing solar power and making it more affordable and accessible to consumers. The company's innovative business model and focus on customer service helped to reduce the barriers to solar adoption and make solar power a viable option for a wider range of homeowners and businesses.

SolarCity's legacy can be seen in the rapid growth of the solar energy market in recent years. Solar power is now one of the fastest-growing energy sources in the world, and SolarCity's pioneering work helped to make this possible.

Specific Examples

Here are some specific examples of how SolarCity's business model and approach helped it to meet the needs of its customers:

- SolarCity's lease-to-own model made solar power more affordable for homeowners and businesses by eliminating the need for a large upfront investment.

- SolarCity's focus on customer service made it easy for customers to switch to solar power. The company provided a hassle-free experience, from the initial consultation to the installation and maintenance of the solar panels.

- SolarCity's commitment to sustainability appealed to customers who were concerned about the environment. The company used only the highest quality solar panels and inverters, and it offered a variety of sustainability features, such as energy monitoring and battery storage.

Overall, SolarCity's story is a testament to the power of innovation and the importance of understanding market needs. By developing a disruptive business model and focusing on customer service and sustainability, SolarCity helped to make solar power more accessible and affordable, and it played a significant role in popularizing solar energy and accelerating its adoption.

Highlight: The concept behind SolarCity was straightforward yet revolutionary: provide, install, and maintain solar panels for residential and commercial customers, thereby removing the barriers to adopting renewable energy. The company's trajectory demonstrates the critical importance of understanding market needs, identifying gaps, and innovating to create financially viable solutions that also deliver substantial societal value.

CHAPTER 11:

Reaching Your Audience: Messaging Strategies

In the dynamic world of startups, amidst the cacophony of competing voices and the frantic hustle to capture market share, the power of precise messaging is paramount. A robust GTM strategy isn't just about having an innovative product or service; it's about articulating its value in a manner that resonates, compels, and persuades. This chapter explores the intricacies of constructing a messaging strategy that not only reaches your target audience but also ignites action and loyalty.

In *Crossing the Chasm*, Geoffrey Moore (2014) delves deep into the challenges startups face when transitioning from serving early adopters to capturing the mainstream market. He emphasizes that while early adopters are more forgiving and willing to overlook product imperfections in favor of innovation, the mainstream market demands a polished, reliable product that fits seamlessly into their lives.

This chasm between the two markets is where many startups falter. They often struggle to communicate the value of their product to a broader audience that doesn't necessarily share the same enthusiasm as the early adopters. This transition underscores the pivotal role of an effective messaging strategy. To bridge this chasm, startups must craft a message that resonates with the pragmatic concerns of the mainstream market, emphasizing reliability, value, and ease of use..

At its core, an effective messaging strategy is a blueprint for articulating your product or service's value clearly, concisely, and persuasively. As Al Ries and Jack Trout (2001) argue in *Positioning: The Battle for Your Mind*, in a world awash with information, the challenge isn't about being louder but more distinct. And this distinction starts with an adept messaging strategy:

- **Identifying and Understanding Your Audience**: As Seth Godin highlights in *This Is Marketing*, it's vital to focus on the smallest viable market segment that can sustain your startup rather than trying to cater to everyone. Understanding your audience, their desires, pain points, and what resonates with them, allows for more tailored and effective messaging.

- **Differentiation from the Competition**: In a saturated market, standing out is indispensable. As emphasized Ries and Trout in *Positioning*, your messaging should etch a unique space in the minds of your consumers. By emphasizing what sets you apart, you're not just selling a product or service, but a unique position in the market landscape.

- **Building Trust and Credibility**: Transparent and forthright messaging fosters trust, ensuring that prospects not only hear your message but believe in it. Furthermore, understanding and delivering the "whole product concept," as argued by Moore, ensures that your offerings meet the comprehensive needs of your target audience, further solidifying trust.

- **Lead Generation and Sales Conversion**: Persuasive messaging, rooted in the needs and aspirations of your target audience, is more likely to inspire action. When your messaging reflects solutions (clearly addressing people's problems), it naturally prompts your audience to engage.

The journey from understanding your audience to generating leads requires a methodical approach. It needs to be a systematic and sustained effort:

- **Grasping Audience Dynamics**: Delve deep into understanding your audience's needs and pain points using surveys, interviews, and focus groups, remembering the difference between early adopters and broader market. Catering to these different segments requires nuanced messaging.

- **Articulating the Value Proposition**: Define what's unique about your offering and how it addresses the needs of your audience.

- **Crafting Key Messages**: Ensure your messages occupy a distinct, memorable space in your audience's mind. They should resonate deeply with their desires and problems.

- **Choosing Effective Communication Channels**: Align your channel strategy with where your audience spends their time. Whether it's social media, email marketing, or paid advertising, the medium is as vital as the message.

- **Content Planning**: An emphasis on creating experiences and stories aligns with this step. Craft content that doesn't just inform, but engages and resonates.

- **Measuring and Adapting**: A dynamic approach is key. Continually measure your outcomes and adjust your strategies. This iterative process ensures that your messaging remains relevant and effective.

Crafting Compelling Content

Once you have clarified your key messages and value proposition, the next step is developing content that brings your messaging to life. Your content strategy should aim to create experiences and stories that engage your audience rather than just provide information.

Here are some tips for creating compelling content:

- Focus on storytelling and visuals: Leverage stories, metaphors, and visuals to connect with your audience on an emotional level and convey complex ideas simply. For example, Slack uses witty comics to explain its features.

- Tailor content to stages of the customer journey: Target content topics to where customers are in their journey, such as awareness, consideration, conversion. For example, educational content for prospects versus product update emails for current users.

- Demonstrate your value proposition: Develop content like case studies, ROI calculators, and product demos that let you show rather than just tell your value proposition.

- Spotlight customer success: User testimonials, reviews, and interviews powerfully convey the real-world impact of your offering.

- Share your purpose and vision: Content on your company's origin story, mission, and vision helps audiences connect with your brand on a deeper level.

- Prioritize mobile and visual: With increasing consumption on mobile, focus on shorter, visual, and interactive content optimized for mobile devices.

- Analyze performance data: Tools like Google Analytics reveal which content best engages your audience. Double down on what works.

- Experiment and iterate: Continuously test new content formats, topics, and channels to refine your approach.

An effective content strategy is not a one-and-done effort. It requires continual optimization based on audience data and feedback. But with compelling content rooted in your core messaging, you can craft experiences that grab attention and drive action.

So, there are several reasons why a messaging strategy is vitally important for startups. First, it helps you to reach your target audience. If you don't know who your target audience is, you can't communicate with them effectively. That is stating the obvious, but a lot of new ventures fail to heed this basic advice. An effective messaging strategy helps you to identify your target audience and understand their needs, interests, and pain points—allowing you to tailor your messaging accordingly.

Second, a messaging strategy helps you to differentiate your product or service from the competition. In a saturated market, it is important to be able to stand out from the crowd. A messaging strategy can help you to do this by highlighting the unique benefits of your product or service. They need to understand how you are different – but in ways that are meaningful and useful.

Third, a messaging strategy helps you to build trust and credibility with your audience. This is absolutely key. If you are honest, transparent, and informative in your messaging, your audience will be more likely to trust you and do business with you.

Ultimately, an effective messaging strategy drives lead generation and sales. Clear, concise, and compelling messaging prompts your audience to engage, whether that's by visiting your website, subscribing to your email list, or making a purchase. Most crucially, you must sidestep the "curse of knowledge." Embrace your target customer's viewpoint to craft messages that resonate deeply, steering clear of jargon and avoiding the pitfalls of "science-speak."

Overcoming the Curse of Knowledge

One of the biggest challenges in developing a messaging strategy is overcoming the curse of knowledge. This cognitive bias refers to the tendency of experts to overestimate the knowledge and understanding of others. In other words, experts often forget what it was like not to know what they know.

This can be a problem when it comes to communicating with your target audience. If you're too focused on the technical details of your product or service, you may forget to explain the basics in a way that your audience can understand.

To overcome the curse of knowledge, it's important to empathize with your target audience. Put yourself in their shoes and consider their level of understanding about your field. Use this perspective to guide your communication.

Indeed, it's important to be clear and concise. This means using simple language that your audience can understand and avoiding jargon unless it's absolutely necessary. If you do use technical terms, be sure to define them clearly. You can also use visuals like diagrams, charts, and images to help illustrate your points.

Here are some specific tips for overcoming the curse of knowledge:

- Ask yourself: What does my target audience already know about my product or service? What do they need to know to make a decision?

- Use plain language: Avoid jargon and technical terms that your audience may not understand.

- Define terms: If you must use technical terms, be sure to define them clearly.

- Use visuals: Visual aids can be a great way to explain complex concepts in a simple and easy-to-understand way.

- Tell stories: Stories are a powerful way to connect with your audience and make your message more memorable.

- Be empathetic: Put yourself in your audience's shoes and consider their needs and concerns.

So, overcoming the curse of knowledge is key to developing a messaging strategy that is clear, concise, and persuasive for your target audience. Let's now further consider the way in which we can achieve that.

Crafting a Compelling Narrative

Transcending the challenge of the curse of knowledge mandates the crafting of a compelling narrative around your product or service. This narrative isn't just words; it's a bridge, a connection to your audience, enabling them to feel, resonate, and recall your message, all while galvanizing them to action.

Commence with the "Why." What looming problem does your product or service rectify? How does it alleviate pain points, simplify challenges, or augment the quality of life for your customer base?

Venture next into the "How." How does your solution unfurl its magic? What unique attributes or benefits does it bring to the fore, distinguishing it from the noise of the competition?

Conclude with the "Impact." Paint a vivid picture of the transformative potential of your product or service. How does it rewrite narratives, bring forth positive change, and elevate the user experience?

Your narrative should be infused with clarity and brevity while retaining its emotive core and persuasive edge. Such a compelling narrative doesn't just inform; it inspires, triggers emotions, and drives action.

Effective Use of Communication Channels

Armed with a magnetic message, the next quest is distribution – selecting the right channels to broadcast this message to your intended audience. The digital age offers a cornucopia of channels, each with its own advantages:

- **Owned media:** Your proprietary platforms—your website, blog, social media presence, and newsletters. It's where you dictate the narrative, nurturing and engaging your audience consistently.

- **Earned media:** The accolades you earn—media mentions, viral shares, organic endorsements, and referrals. It's the realm of credibility and expanded outreach.

- **Paid media:** Your investments to amplify reach—ads, sponsored content, partnerships with influencers. Here, you pay to play, reaching audiences rapidly and on a grand scale.

(FIGURE 26: DIGITAL MEDIA)

Choosing the right mix hinges on your product's nature, budget considerations, and overarching goals. Nevertheless, an amalgamation of channels usually works best, ensuring a broad and diverse reach.

Yet, it's not just about channel diversity; it's about **consistency**. While it's pivotal to craft a compelling narrative, the power of this narrative is amplified manifold when it's consistently echoed across all communication touchpoints. A seamless, congruent story across channels not only reinforces your brand but also ensures that your message doesn't get diluted or lost in translation. Consistency fortifies your brand voice, ensuring it rings true, clear, and authentic irrespective of where your audience encounters it.

In essence, while being wary of the curse of knowledge, it's paramount to design a message that's not just compelling but also ubiquitously consistent. By crafting a story that's both resonant and reliably replicated across diverse channels, you stand a better chance at etching your brand into the consciousness of your target demographics.

So, let now move on to our case study that showcases the power of a well-crafted messaging strategy by SpaceX, the space exploration agency.

CASE STUDY: SPACEX

SpaceX, founded in 2002 by Elon Musk, is a private space exploration company with the mission to make life multi-planetary. SpaceX has disrupted the space industry by developing reusable rocket technology that has dramatically reduced the cost of space travel. The company has also pioneered a number of other innovations, such as the Falcon 9 rocket and the Dragon spacecraft.

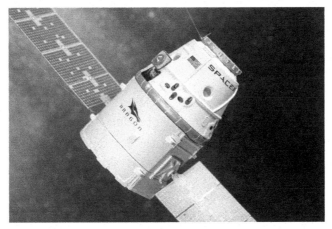

(FIGURE 27: SPACEX)

One of the key factors in SpaceX's success has been its clear and compelling messaging strategy. The company has been able to articulate its vision and mission in a way that has resonated with its audience, both internally and externally. This has helped SpaceX to attract top talent and build a strong following among the public.

SpaceX's messaging is centered around the following key themes:

- Making space travel more affordable and accessible: SpaceX believes that space travel should be available to everyone, not just a select few. The company's reusable rocket technology is helping to make this a reality.

- Exploring the solar system and beyond: SpaceX is committed to expanding human presence in space. The company is developing Starship, a reusable rocket system that is designed to transport humans and cargo to the Moon, Mars, and beyond.

- Making life multi-planetary: SpaceX believes that humans have a future beyond Earth. The company is working to make it possible for humans to live and thrive on other planets.

SpaceX's messaging has been effective in reaching its target audience, which includes young people, entrepreneurs, and anyone who is interested in space exploration. The company has a strong presence on social media, and it regularly releases videos and other content that is designed to inspire and educate the public.

For example, SpaceX's "Inspiration4" mission, which launched in September 2021, was the first all-civilian mission to orbit Earth. The mission was widely covered by the media, and it helped to generate excitement about SpaceX and its mission.

SpaceX's messaging has also been effective in attracting top talent. The company is known for its innovative culture and its ambitious goals. This has attracted a large pool of talented engineers and scientists who are drawn to the opportunity to work on cutting-edge space technology.

Overall, SpaceX's messaging strategy has been a key factor in its success. The company has been able to articulate its vision and mission in a way that has resonated with its target audience, and it has used this messaging to attract top talent and build a strong following among the public.

Highlight: SpaceX is a model for how to use messaging effectively to reach your target audience and achieve your goals. The company's clear, compelling, and consistent messaging has helped it to attract top talent, build a strong following among the public, and disrupt the space industry.

CHAPTER 12:
Building Your Team for Success

Introduction

Building an effective team is one of the most vital yet challenging aspects of launching a successful startup. While the capabilities required evolve across a startup's developmental stages, one reality remains constant – a startup's destiny lies in the hands of its people.

This chapter takes a comprehensive look at the nuances of assembling teams optimized for startup success. We'll explore relevant organizational behavior theories to shed light on group dynamics. We'll consider team composition across various stages of the startup lifecycle. While the team requirements morph as the company grows, the founding team DNA imprints cultural elements that persist.

Of course, core startup activities necessitate specialized competencies at each phase. As startups approach go-to-market execution, the team equation becomes particularly complex. This stage demands a balancing act, requiring both commercial acumen and retention of the founders' mentality that powered the initial breakthrough innovation. We will delve into the unique considerations of building a team tailored for go-to-market excellence.

By peering into the psychology of teams through an organizational behavior lens, and understanding the shifting demands of various startup stages, founders can deliberately create winning, high-performing teams. Your team composition will encounter unanticipated twists, but with agility and foresight, you can assemble the perfect ensemble to ascend from scrappy startup to scaled-up juggernaut.

The Founding Team

The nucleus of any startup is its founding team. This core group is entrusted with the monumental tasks of setting the company's vision, crafting its strategy, and executing its plans. They are the torchbearers who attract investors, build the team, and lay the foundation for the company's culture.

A few non-negotiable traits define an effective founding team. Firstly, an intimate understanding of the startup's technology or science is paramount. This isn't just about developing the product or service; it's about articulating the company's value proposition to potential customers and investors.

Leadership is the second pillar. Founding members should be adept at motivating and inspiring others, making challenging decisions, adapting to change, and managing priorities, all while under immense pressure.

Thirdly, an unwavering passion for the startup's mission is essential. This translates to long hours, sacrifices, and a steadfast commitment to the startup's long-term vision.

However, beyond these foundational traits, diversity in skills and experiences is a game-changer. Such diversity fosters creative thinking, problem-solving, and a nuanced understanding of the target market. Consider a startup developing a medical device. A team comprising engineers, scientists, and business professionals would be ideal. While engineers provide technical expertise, scientists ensure the device's safety and efficacy, and business professionals navigate its market journey.

Airbnb's success story is a testament to the power of a diverse founding team. Their varied backgrounds and perspectives have been instrumental in the company's meteoric rise.

Seasoned investors and entrepreneurs recognize the significance of a harmonious, skilled, and diverse team. Such a team can transform a brilliant idea into a flourishing business, weather storms, and rebound from setbacks. In contrast, a team lacking in chemistry or skills can hinder innovation, succumb to challenges, or let egos derail progress.

An academic startup's heart and soul are its academic founders and researchers. These individuals, be they professors, post-docs, or graduate students, infuse the startup with scientific prowess. Yet, as they transition into the startup world, they grapple with unfamiliar terrain—strategic planning, investor relations, marketing, sales, and legal intricacies.

Bridging the chasm between technical knowledge and business savvy necessitates a balanced team, grounded in diversity, chemistry, and a spectrum of complementary skills.

Entrepreneurs are constantly engaged in building internal resources and capabilities. They leverage partnerships and manage the intricate dance between resources, partners, and strategic actions. As young ventures strive for growth, they must not only build on their resources but also outmaneuver competitors. The iterative process of resource building and leveraging is crucial.

Sometimes, building internal capabilities and forging partnerships can be alternatives, but both can dictate the strategic actions available to boost revenue and profits. These actions, in turn, mold future resources and capabilities. All these maneuvers occur in varied competitive landscapes, influencing the efficacy of different approaches to resource building, partnering, and action-taking.

As startups evolve, entrepreneurs must transcend their initial conditions. This often means integrating new talent into the venture and organizing them optimally. A pressing question arises: When is the right time to bring in new people? Should one wait for the perfect moment to fully leverage new hires, or should the hiring process be more immediate? Research indicates (Combes et al, 2023) that proactive hiring, done as soon as a skill gap is identified, propels growth. In contrast, a more cautious, incremental approach tends to fuel slower growth. The message is clear: for rapid growth, hire promptly when new skills are needed.

Having established the importance of timely hiring and the strategic integration of diverse skills into a startup, it's essential to delve deeper into the nuances of team composition. Beyond the tangible skills and experiences, the intangible elements—like personality traits—play a pivotal role in shaping the dynamics of a startup team. Recognizing and understanding these traits can be the difference between a harmonious, productive team and one riddled with conflicts and inefficiencies. This brings us to the intricate realm of personality and its profound impact on team building and entrepreneurial success.

Personality Traits

The complexity of human nature means that there is no one-size-fits-all blueprint for team composition. Although understanding of personality theory—such as the Big Five traits and their impact on motivation and behavior—can be a helpful starting point, it can't provide an infallible formula. Having said that, being aware of these diverse personality traits and their influence on work styles and team dynamics can steer us clear of common pitfalls, increasing the chances of assembling a team that aligns with the startup's needs and culture.

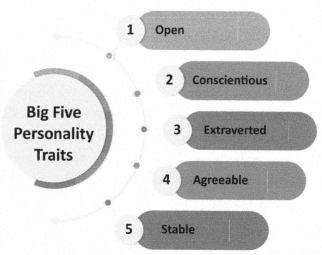

(FIGURE 28: THE BIG FIVE PERSONALITY TRAITS)

According to recent academic literature, there are several proposed frameworks suggesting key success factors for new ventures. These include the fundamental importance of the core idea, the style of leadership, the business model, and the marketing philosophy. However, the entrepreneurial team's competency and composition are often underscored as decisive factors. The interplay between these "hard" factors and the "soft" dynamics of the team is crucial for the venture's success.

This chapter will explore the critical elements of building a winning team for your startup, thereby facilitating a smooth transition from academia to the entrepreneurial world. We'll delve into the characteristics of the founding team, the essence of a balanced team, the crucial role of team chemistry, and the importance of diversity. Through examining how these elements interact and reinforce one another, we aim to provide valuable insights that will set the stage for your startup's successful growth, starting from the required mindset.

Founder Mindset

In their book *The Founder's Mentality*, Bain & Company's Chris Zook and James Allen (2016) argue that the founder's mentality is essential for startups. They define the founder's mentality as "a mindset that allows a company to maintain its agility and focus on the customer experience, even as it grows and scales." The authors suggest that there are three key elements that underpin this mentality:

- A focus on the customer: Startups need to be obsessed with their customers and their needs. They need to constantly be listening to feedback and iterating on their products and services to ensure that they are meeting those needs. This is especially important in the early stages of a startup when the company is still trying to figure out who its customers are and what they need.

- A bias for action: Startups need to be willing to take risks and experiment. They can't afford to wait for all the data or perfect the product before they launch. They need to get their products and services out there and start learning from their customers. This is essential for startups to be able to quickly adapt to changing market conditions.

- A sense of urgency: Startups need to be constantly moving forward. They can't afford to rest on their laurels. They need to be constantly innovating and looking for new ways to grow. This is essential for startups to stay ahead of the competition.

So, the founding team can play a key role in instilling a winning mentality in a startup. It should be composed of people who share the foundational mindset and who are passionate about the company's mission. Their responsibilities are varied, from setting the company's vision and strategy to executing its plans.

But their role doesn't stop there; they are also instrumental in wooing investors, assembling a robust team, and cultivating the company's culture. Given the significance of entrepreneurial competencies discussed earlier, it becomes evident that the competency of the founding team is paramount, especially during the nascent stages of an academic startup's journey.

So, what are the core characteristics that a founding team should have? Well, these can be distilled to four key areas:

- Technical or domain expertise: The founding team must have a deep understanding of the startup's technology or science. This knowledge is essential for developing the product or service, communicating the company's value proposition, and attracting investors.

- Strong sense of mission: The founding team must be passionate about the startup's mission. This passion will drive them to work hard and overcome challenges. They must be willing to put in long hours and make sacrifices for the company's success.

- Agility and adaptability: The founding team must be able to adapt to change and pivot as needed. The startup environment is constantly changing, and the founding team must be able to keep up. This means being able to quickly identify and respond to new opportunities and challenges.

- Complementary skills and experience: The founding team should have a variety of skills and experience that complement each other. This will allow them to cover all aspects of the business and make better decisions.

As startups evolve, their needs change, requiring periodic reassessment of team composition. Just like phase transitions in physics, which mark a shift from one state of matter to another (e.g., solid to liquid) with a radical change in system dynamics, startups undergo their own "phase transitions."

Each growth stage of a startup introduces distinct challenges and demands. To navigate these shifts effectively, the founding team must be agile, recalibrating their composition to align with the company's current needs. In the nascent stages, the emphasis might be on product development, requiring a team rich in innovation and technical prowess.

As the startup matures, the spotlight shifts to sales and marketing, more formalized human resource structures—all of which demand a different skill set. Further down the line, high level financial and operational expertise become paramount. In essence, the team's composition isn't static; it's a dynamic interplay of parts, evolving in tandem with the startup's journey.

Enter the Business Professionals

As a startup evolves and progresses through different stages of its lifecycle, the intensity and complexity of its business operations expand. The initial stages, often steeped in innovation and technology development, are driven by the guidance of academic founders and research personnel. And as the startup matures, its needs diversify and intensify, necessitating specialized expertise across a broad spectrum of business domains—financial, sales and marketing, supply chain, HR, etc.

During this critical transition, integrating seasoned business professionals into the team becomes a strategic imperative. However, this can also pose a dilemma. On the one hand, these professionals bring valuable experience and expertise that can help the startup scale and grow. On the other hand, there is a danger that they may dilute the founding team's original vision and culture.

To mitigate this risk, it is important to carefully select the right business professionals for the team. They should be aligned with the startup's vision and mission, and they should be willing to buy into the founding team's culture. They should also be able to add value to the team in terms of their skills and experience.

One vital role that stands at the heart of successful growth-oriented startups is the Chief Revenue Officer (CRO). The titles may vary—Chief Growth Officer, Chief Commercial Officer, Chief Experience Officer, among others—but the core responsibilities remain. He or she is entrusted with orchestrating a comprehensive revenue engine, encompassing everything from lead generation through digital marketing to closing sales. The role transcends traditional sales and marketing boundaries to incorporate the broader market context, customer journey, and strategic expansion plans. So, it does not replace these functions; it adds an additional strategic, integrative layer.

CROs are adept at understanding every aspect of customer acquisition and retention. They align people, processes, and technology across the entire revenue cycle, harmonizing people, data, and metrics across sales and marketing teams. Generative AI models are spurring a major transformation in marketing, sales, and revenue-generating activities. As these AI technologies progress, startups should continually strive to use AI-powered tools to streamline workflows and drive growth. As automation increases, an agile and adaptive strategy is required to avoid being overtaken by competitors.

Dunbar's Number

Startups are inherently growth-oriented, but as they expand, they face new challenges, such as complex team dynamics and a diluted founder's mindset. This is where Dunbar's Number, a fascinating theory proposed by British anthropologist and Oxford University Professor Robin Dunbar, becomes highly relevant to understanding the changing dynamics of growth.

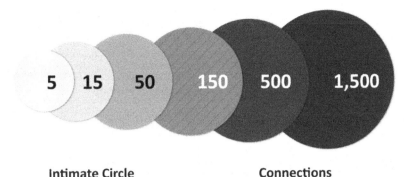

Intimate Circle   Connections

(FIGURE 29: DUNBAR'S NUMBER)

Dunbar's Number is a theoretical limit to the number of people with whom one can maintain stable social relationships. He estimated this number to be around 150 for humans. This means that a startup with a team of more than 150 people will find it difficult to maintain close relationships and coordination between all team members.

This can lead to a number of challenges, such as:

- Communication becomes more complex and impersonal.
- Decision-making becomes more difficult and time-consuming.
- Trust becomes harder to build and maintain.
- Productivity may suffer.

To mitigate these challenges, it is important for startups to be mindful of Dunbar's Number and to take steps to build strong relationships and coordination within their teams. This may involve creating smaller, more intimate teams, or using technology to facilitate communication and collaboration across larger teams.

Motivating and Engaging the Team

Employee motivation and engagement are pivotal in any organization, as detailed in my book *Engaging the Workforce: The Grand Management Challenge of the 21st* Century (Rossides, 2023). The dynamics become particularly delicate and complex within academic startups, especially as they transition through the startup's life cycle.

In the initial stages, an academic startup often comprises a small team: the founder, co-founder, and perhaps a research associate. Here, the challenge is self-motivation and perseverance. Grappling with the challenges of a considerable workload, initially in combination with academic responsibilities. However, as the startup expands, the team's growth introduces complexities reminiscent of larger, established entities.

As the team evolves, so does its nature. New members introduce opportunities for enhanced engagement and productivity. And engaged employees (characterized by *vigor, dedication* and *absorption*) are indispensable, driving the company's culture and ethos.

Yet, growth is a double-edged sword. As the startup matures, it faces challenges akin to larger organizations. To navigate these challenges, several strategies emerge:

- **Delegation:** Essential for growth, delegation allows leaders to focus on overarching goals.

- **Clarity:** Defining roles and expectations streamlines processes. Modern communication tools can further enhance clarity.

- **Trust:** Strengthened through shared experiences, trust is foundational for team cohesion.

- **Transparency:** An open culture ensures everyone feels involved and valued.

These strategies gain prominence as the team expands. While the concept of Dunbar's Number provides a lens to view potential scaling challenges, a mix of proactive measures ensures growth is a boon, not a bane.

Furthermore, academic startups, rooted in university settings, prioritize research and academic values. But in the commercial sphere, a cohesive and dynamic culture is what is needed. Collaboration and common workflows over the individual effort in the quest for accolades for ourselves.

Building a Positive Culture

When dealing with the dynamic context of startups, we need to keep in mind that culture isn't merely a backdrop; it's foundational. Culture emerges from shared experiences and learned solutions to the team's problems. It's the assumptions we don't see that powerfully influence our behavior (Schein 2010).

At the heart of a positive culture is trust—it underlies the shared basic assumptions. It allows open communication, facilitating "double-loop learning," a term coined by Harvard's late professor Chris Argyris in his classic "On Organizational Learning" (Argyris 1999). This entails not just fixing errors, but understanding and modifying the underlying norms and values causing those errors. When team members deeply trust each other, they engage in more than just problem-solving; they embrace genuine reflection and growth.

A potent startup culture embraces a shared vision. This isn't about conformity but about unity of purpose. When every team member sees their role not as a cog in the machine but as a vital contributor to the broader mission, this catalyzes engagement and innovation. And this aligns well with Schein's belief that the beliefs driving our actions often operate at an unconscious level. In other words, they're deeply embedded, forming the core of the organization.

Yet, even a deeply entrenched culture must possess a chameleon-like adaptability. The journey of a startup is rife with unpredictability. As external challenges arise, the internal culture must evolve—and here the idea of organizational learning is key, emphasizing the need for organizations to continually adapt and learn to stay relevant.

Further strengthening the cultural fabric, the following managerial practices may be helpful:

- **Celebrate as One**: Achievements, as Schein would argue, are shared experiences that further embed culture. Celebrate them to fortify bonds.

- **Diversity**: Argyris often stressed the value of diverse perspectives for effective learning. A varied team brings richer, multifaceted insights.

- **Connection**: Growth, in Argyris's view, is as much about learning from mistakes as from feedback. A culture that welcomes feedback ensures it remains vibrant and responsive.

- **Humility**: Schein believed that leaders must be humble learners, always curious. This openness invites collective wisdom and shapes culture from within.

So, startups must weave a culture that's grounded in trust, unified in purpose, and resilient in the face of change—and a core aspect of this culture is a continued effort to learn and develop our human capital. Indeed, in a rapidly changing world, startups must be agile, and at the heart of this agility is the commitment to nurturing and developing human capital.

Continuous Learning & Development

As we delve deeper into the significance of competencies, as the foundation of a strong culture, it becomes evident that their importance isn't static. As a startup evolves and matures, so too do the competencies it requires. As we've already discussed in detail, the advent of digitalization and AI has revolutionized the way we work. While they automate and enhance routine tasks, they simultaneously elevate the complexity of other cognitive processes—which means that the competencies employees once relied on might quickly become obsolete.

Recognizing this, leading organizations, governments, and firms across the globe have taken proactive measures. They understand that to stay competitive, they must equip their workforce with the competencies that today's labor market demands. The World Economic Forum's data underscores this shift, revealing that approximately two-thirds of global multinational organizations are investing in reskilling their current employees. This isn't just a trend; it's a strategic move to future-proof their workforce in light of the dramatic short-ening of the shelf-life of competencies.

Conclusion

Building a robust team is akin to composing a symphony – you need instru-ments capable of hitting the right notes, playing in harmony. As a startup evolves, the sheet music changes, requiring different instrumentation. The core persists – a shared vision, chemistry, motivation – but the specifics must adapt.

While team composition follows no rigid formula, certain tenets hold significance:

- Assemble technically-adept founders with business acumen and leadership abilities.
- Blend complementary capabilities in areas like sales, marketing, and analytics.
- Maintain flexibility to pivot as needs change.

At the go-to-market stage, the tempo accelerates, necessitating key hires in cus-tomer-facing roles. However, the original founders must retain strategic influ-ence, ensuring the startup maintains its core identity even as it commercializes.

There will be dissonant notes and triumphant crescendos. But remember, today's virtuoso was once an uncertain novice. With a willingness to learn and adapt, plus commitment to your talent, your startup's team can orchestrate growth and achieve true harmony.

Now, before we pivot to our next chapter on the Go-To-Market Toolkit for academic startups, let's examine the case of Apple, a company that exemplifies cultural excellence in action.

CASE STUDY: APPLE

From its humble beginnings in a garage in 1976, Apple has grown to become a global technology powerhouse, largely due to its outstanding team. The company's founders—Steve Jobs, Steve Wozniak, and Ronald Wayne—knew that to realize their vision, they needed to assemble a team with a similar mindset and complementary skill sets.

(FIGURE 30: APPLE)

Apple's success story is a testament to the power of building a world-class team. The company's founders—Steve Jobs and Steve Wozniak—had complementary skills and a shared vision, but their relationship was not without its challenges. Jobs' demanding personality and Wozniak's more laid-back style sometimes led to conflict.

Despite their differences, Jobs and Wozniak were able to work together effectively to create some of the most iconic products in history. Their collaboration was instrumental in Apple's early success and helped to lay the foundation for the company's continued dominance of the tech industry.

In addition to Jobs and Wozniak, Apple's early team included other talented individuals such as Ronald Wayne, Jef Raskin, and Bill Atkinson. These individuals played key roles in developing Apple's early products, such as the Apple II and the Macintosh.

Expanding the Team to Meet New Challenges

As Apple grew and expanded into new markets, the company's team evolved accordingly. In recent years, Apple has made significant investments in artificial intelligence, machine learning, and augmented reality. This has led to the recruitment of top talent in these fields, further strengthening Apple's team and enabling it to continue to innovate.

Apple's commitment to building a world-class team is evident in its diverse workforce. The company employs people from all walks of life, with a wide range of backgrounds, experiences, and perspectives. This diversity is a valuable asset for Apple, as it sparks innovation and helps the company to better understand and meet the needs of its global customer base.

Creating a Culture of Innovation and Collaboration

Apple's team culture is one of innovation and collaboration. Employees are encouraged to think outside the box and challenge the status quo. They are also given the resources and support they need to bring their ideas to life.

One of the key ways that Apple fosters innovation is through its focus on design. Apple's design team is world-renowned for its ability to create products that are both beautiful and functional. Apple's designers work closely with engineers and other team members to ensure that every product meets the company's high standards for design and quality.

Apple also encourages collaboration across different teams. This is facilitated by the company's unique organizational structure, which places the CEO at the center of all major decisions. This allows for rapid communication and decision-making, which is essential in the fast-paced tech industry.

Highlight: Apple's success is a testament to the power of building a world-class team. Despite differences in personality and managerial style, Jobs and Wozniak were able to work together effectively to create some of the most iconic products in history. Apple has continued to invest in building a team of the best and brightest minds in the tech industry. The company's focus on innovation and collaboration have helped to create a team that is capable of developing groundbreaking products and services that change the way people live and work.

CHAPTER 13:
Measuring & Iterating: The Evidence Base

In the unpredictable world of startups, measuring and refining your go-to-market strategy is akin to a reliable compass guiding you toward sustained growth. But it's crucial to discern between being data-driven and evidence-driven. Both require agility and a commitment to continuous learning, but I lean towards "evidence-based" because it emphasizes informed and deliberate decision-making.

Data, when looked at in isolation, are just raw facts or figures. On the other hand, evidence provides context, offering insights that can either support or refute a conclusion. An evidence-based approach goes beyond raw data, adding layers of interpretation and actionable insights. So, in this chapter, our focus will be on collecting and applying evidence to shape our GTM strategy. We'll delve into defining success through Key Performance Indicators (KPIs) and then discuss refining your GTM strategy based on the insights these KPIs provide (Also, see Appendix B).

Data is a valuable tool in navigating the uncertain waters of startups, but it should guide rather than dominate your decisions. There's a real danger in getting stuck in "analysis paralysis," where an overload of data can stifle action. While metrics provide a clear picture, blending them with foresight and innovative problem-solving is equally vital. Remember, just because two things correlate doesn't mean one caused the other. It's essential to measure what genuinely impacts your startup's success.

Here, the Pareto Principle or the 80/20 rule can be a guiding light. It suggests that 80% of your outcomes come from just 20% of your efforts. By focusing on this crucial 20%, you can achieve most of your desired results.

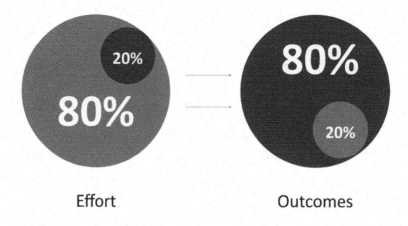

Effort   Outcomes

(FIGURE 31: THE PARETO PRINCIPLE)

However, not every situation demands perfection. Sometimes, a "satisficing" approach, which aims for adequacy rather than complete optimization, is more practical. With this foundation, let's explore how we can define success and the nuances of iterative refinement.

Defining Success (KPIs)

At the heart of any Go-To-Market strategy lies a clear definition of success, often articulated through Key Performance Indicators (KPIs). These quantifiable metrics resonate with your strategic aims and act as your business's heartbeat, spotlighting strengths and areas needing attention.

The KPIs you choose should align with your business model, strategic objectives, and the stage of your startup. For a GTM strategy, typical KPIs might include Market Share, Sales Growth, Customer Acquisition Cost (CAC), Customer Lifetime Value (CLV), and Net Promoter Score (NPS).

To foster continuous growth, consider adopting Objectives and Key Results (OKRs), a renowned goal-setting framework. It pairs ambitious objectives with measurable steps (Key Results) to achieve them. Some organizations even blend the OKR approach with the SMART criteria, ensuring goals are ambitious yet Specific, Measurable, Achievable, Relevant, and Time-bound.

(FIGURE 32: SMART & OKRS)

OKRs are ideal when you're chasing ambitious goals, often associated with rapid growth. In contrast, SMART goals are more suited to situations focusing on continuous improvement.

When merging the two, you might set a SMART goal as your primary objective, then define Key Results as OKRs, setting ambitious targets that propel you towards that goal.

Selecting KPIs: Horses for Courses

The phrase "horses for courses" comes to mind when considering KPIs. Many founders set their KPIs based on arbitrary or generic goals without considering their startup's life stage and their strategy. As your business evolves, so will your strategies, and your KPIs should reflect that. It's essential to be realistic about your resources and capabilities. If your primary KPI isn't growing or declines for three consecutive months, it's a sign that something's off. You might need to pivot or even consider shutting down. Y Combinator, the world's largest accelerator, uses this rule weekly. If a startup doesn't show growth for three weeks, they're advised to pivot or contemplate closure.

To illustrate, during the MVP stage, startups might focus on KPIs like average customer reviews, retention rate, revenue per client, and Customer Acquisition Cost (CAC). Post Business Model Validation, the emphasis might shift to Customer Lifetime Value (LTV), user growth rate, transaction growth rate, revenue growth rate, and the ratio of gross margin to expenses.

So, there are some key considerations when selecting your KPIs:

- Align KPIs with your startup's stage: Early-stage startups may focus more on leads and conversions, while later-stage companies track CLV and churn rate.

- Limit your KPIs: Tracking too many metrics can lead to confusion. Focus on 1-2 KPIs per strategic goal.

- Make KPIs actionable: KPIs should connect to specific activities so you know how to influence them.

- Balance lagging and leading indicators: Lagging indicators (revenue, profit) show past performance while leading indicators (web traffic, leads) signal future performance.

- Benchmark KPIs: Evaluate your KPIs relative to competitors or industry averages.

- Regularly review KPIs: As your business evolves, your KPIs need to as well. Don't stick with outdated metrics.

- Automate tracking: Use tools to automatically monitor your KPIs through integrated dashboards. This provides real-time visibility.

Selecting the right KPIs for your startup's strategic objectives and life cycle stage is crucial. This not only defines success but steers your business decisions and growth trajectory.

Iterating Your Strategy: Rinse & Repeat

The concept of iterative refinement lies at the heart of the Lean Startup methodology, and it is equally indispensable to your GTM strategy—and the

KPIs you select to track its successful implementation. It allows frequent adjustments to your strategy based on performance data, customer feedback, and revenue indicators, transforming your strategy into a constant learning process on what works and what does not.

The iterative process may involve refining your product features, adjusting your pricing, adapting your marketing tactics, or sometimes, pivoting your entire business model. A critical part of this process is to build a robust revenue engine that aligns marketing, sales, and customer success. This revenue focus is a key component of the iterative approach but needs to be fine-tuned according to the ventures stage in its lifecycle. It revolves around understanding customer behaviors, preferences, and needs, and optimizing marketing and sales strategies to maximize revenue at key stages in its evolution.

At its core, the iterative strategy fosters adaptability, embraces changes, and promotes a culture of continuous learning from both victories and setbacks. It's a dynamic cycle that keeps customer-centric revenue generation at its heart, ensuring that the focus remains firmly on creating value for the customer and driving sustainable growth for the business.

In the startup ecosystem, your GTM strategy is not a fixed plan but a dynamic blueprint that evolves with your business, always aiming for optimal customer satisfaction and revenue growth. The most successful startups are those that pivot, adapt, and refine their strategies as required, incorporating changes, continuous learning, and a relentless pursuit of revenue generation into their growth pathway.

Some best practices for an effective iterative approach include:

- Establish rapid feedback loops: Quickly gather customer insights through surveys, interviews, beta tests.
- Analyze cohort data: Track how different customer segments behave over time.
- Run frequent A/B tests: Test variations of messaging, pricing, features etc. to see what resonates.

- Monitor real-time analytics: Tools like Mixpanel provide granular data on user behavior.

- Review funnel metrics: Identify blockages preventing customers from converting.

- Hold regular strategy reviews: Frequently re-evaluate your GTM strategy and refine as needed.

- Foster a test-and-learn culture: Accept failures and missteps as learnings to improve.

- Share insights cross-functionally: Ensure insights from tests or pilots are shared across teams.

- Automate where possible: Automating repetitive tasks frees you up for strategic initiatives.

So, an iterative, evidence-based approach is crucial as your startup evolves and new challenges emerge. Continuously optimizing your GTM strategy based on the latest customer and market data is what will keep you ahead of the curve

Let's now examine how Dropbox grew into a hugely successful company by using evidence-based decision-making and pivoting when necessary.

CASE STUDY: DROPBOX

When Dropbox first launched in 2007, it offered a simple value proposition: making files accessible anywhere. Initially targeting individual users, the company grew rapidly. By early 2011, Dropbox was home to 25 million users.

(FIGURE 33: DROPBOX)

However, Dropbox's team noticed an interesting pattern in their user data; a significant portion of their users were utilizing Dropbox for business-related purposes. Indeed, a study they conducted found that 40% of businesses were using Dropbox to store and share files. This realization sparked a series of questions. What if Dropbox could serve these users even better by tailoring a product specifically for them?

With these insights in hand, the Dropbox team decided to experiment. They developed a new product named Dropbox for Teams (later renamed to Dropbox for Business) and initiated a closed beta program. The intent was to validate their hypothesis and understand how businesses might use their product differently from individual users.

Data became the guiding light in this journey. Dropbox closely monitored a range of metrics to track the new product's performance. Some key metrics included:

- Number of active teams: In 2021, Dropbox for Business had over 300,000 active teams, up from 100,000 in 2020. This represented a 300% increase in the number of active teams.
- Number of files shared within teams: In 2021, Dropbox for Business users shared over 2.5 trillion files, up from 1 trillion

files in 2020. This represented a 250% increase in the number of files shared.

- Amount of storage used: In 2021, Dropbox for Business users used over 100 petabytes of storage, up from 50 petabytes in 2020. This represented a 100% increase in the amount of storage used.

- Churn rate: The churn rate for Dropbox for Business is below 5%, compared to 10% for individual users. This means that businesses are more likely to stick with Dropbox for Business than individual users.

- Customer lifetime value (CLTV): The CLTV for Dropbox for Business is over $1,000, compared to $500 for individual users. This means that businesses are more profitable customers for Dropbox than individual users.

Their measurements revealed insightful trends. For instance, Dropbox for Business users demonstrated a lower churn rate and a higher CLTV compared to the individual users. These findings supported the notion that the new product offered a more sustainable growth path.

Armed with this data, Dropbox decided to invest more resources into Dropbox for Business, expanding the features to cater more effectively to its business users. The team continued their iterative process, using customer feedback and data to refine and improve their offering. Today, Dropbox for Business forms a significant part of the company's revenue, serving over 300,000 business teams worldwide.

Highlights: Dropbox's journey illustrates the power of evidence-driven decisions and iterative development, leading to a product that now serves hundreds of thousands of business teams worldwide.

The KPIs that Dropbox tracked helped them to make informed decisions about how to improve Dropbox for Business. For example, the low churn rate indicated that businesses were satisfied with the product, so Dropbox focused on adding features that would make it even more valuable to businesses. The high CLTV showed that Dropbox for Business was a profitable product, so Dropbox continued to invest in it.

By tracking the right KPIs, Dropbox was able to grow its business and improve its product. This is a valuable lesson for any startup or business that wants to use data to make better decisions.

CHAPTER 14:
Crafting a Compelling Pitch Deck

Crafting a compelling pitch deck for your startup is akin to composing a song. It requires the right blend of elements—harmony, rhythm, and a catchy melody—to make it memorable. Similarly, your pitch deck needs to hit the right notes to resonate with potential investors. This might seem like a tough task for academic entrepreneurs, especially when trying to communicate your startup's value proposition in a language that investors understand.

If you're like most founders, you probably think about your startup constantly. You live and breathe your idea, from the moment you wake up brainstorming product features, to when you fall asleep with visions of marketing campaigns and business plans dancing in your head. Leisurely activities like watching a movie or reading a book have been replaced by collaborating with developers, fine-tuning your business model, or connecting with potential investors or customers on LinkedIn.

While passion, hard work, and a healthy dose of obsession are vital ingredients to entrepreneurial success, it's not uncommon for founders to become so engrossed in the intricacies of their ideas that they overlook a critical fact: your progress hinges on your ability to pitch the value of your startup convincingly to those who hold the purse strings.

Whether it's raising venture capital, sourcing top talent, or acquiring new customers, these milestones all require the same skill—telling a story that's as clear as it is compelling. It should be a story that resonates. Sometimes, you only have a short window—a 30-minute meeting, or even a fleeting minute in an elevator—to convince someone why they should care about your business.

This chapter will be your guide as we deconstruct the elements of a successful pitch deck. We'll also tackle the curse of knowledge, a cognitive hiccup that can turn your harmonious pitch into a dissonant symphony that frustrates or baffles investors.

Simplicity and Clarity

We've already covered the curse of knowledge—a cognitive bias where an individual, immersed in their field of expertise, inadvertently assumes that others have the same level of understanding. It's a universal affliction and results in either the bewildered audience member or the oblivious presenter at some point in our careers. You might have found yourself diving deep into the mechanics of your innovative technology, only to be met with vacant stares from investors. Or perhaps you've received that polite but ominous "We'll call you" dismissal—an indication that your pitch fell flat.

The antidote to this predicament lies in simplicity, clarity, and focus. While investors might not share your enthusiasm for the intricate details of your innovation, they will be eager to understand its market potential and how it translates into profitability. Remember, the pitch deck is not just about your deep knowledge or the complex science behind your product—it's about the compelling story you craft around it. Now, let's dissect the components of a pitch that truly connects and resonates—one that excites enough to ignite a desire to invest.

A Compelling Pitch Deck

As you prepare to compose your pitch deck, think of it as the storyboard for a movie—each slide is a scene contributing to the overall narrative. Here's a guide to creating a "script" that hits the mark.

Business Model: This is the foundation of your startup story. It's crucial to articulate how your startup creates, delivers, and captures value. Investors need to understand how your business operates and how it will generate revenue. Does your startup follow a subscription model, a transaction fee model, or perhaps a freemium model? Here, it's not just about stating the model but also explaining why it's the best fit for your product and market.

For example, Slack's freemium model not only allowed users to test the service but also demonstrated its value, leading to a high conversion rate to the premium version.

Value Proposition: This is the heart of your story. It's where you explain the unique benefits your product or service provides to your Ideal Customer Profile (ICP) and how it differs from existing alternatives. Make sure to clearly identify the problem you're solving and explain why your solution is not just unique, but superior. For instance, when Uber first started, their value proposition was simple yet compelling: "Tap a button, get a ride." They were offering convenience, efficiency, and an improved riding experience compared to traditional taxis.

Market Analysis: This section is the setting for your story. It's where you showcase your understanding of the market, the problem you are addressing, and your potential share in the market. Here, you need to provide concrete data on market size, growth, and trends. Also, identify your target audience and how your product addresses their needs better than existing solutions. In the case of Netflix, they recognized the shift towards online streaming and understood that their potential market was not just movie watchers but anyone with internet access.

Go-To-Market Strategy: This is your strategic battle plan. It outlines your plan for capturing market share, including your lead generation strategies, conversion rates, and chosen marketing channels. Be specific about your sales and marketing strategies. How will you acquire new customers? What channels will you use to reach them? Investors will look at this section to understand how you plan to grow. For instance, Dropbox's referral program was a critical part of their GTM strategy, helping them grow from 100k users to 4 million users in just 15 months.

Traction: This is your "show, don't tell" slide. Here, you highlight the progress your startup has made to date, such as customer testimonials, sales growth, partnerships, or other forms of validation. Concrete examples of your success are far more compelling than abstract promises. For example, Airbnb showcased their week-over-week growth and the positive reviews from users in their pitch deck, providing tangible proof of their business's potential.

Fund Utilization: This is where you show that you're a responsible steward. You need to detail how you intend to use the funds raised, such as for product development, hiring, marketing, or expansion. Investors want to see that you have a clear plan for their money and that you'll use it judiciously to grow the business. A chart or a graph can be an effective way to communicate this.

Remember, each pitch deck is unique to the company presenting it. For instance, Airbnb's seed round pitch deck provides an excellent example of a concise yet compelling presentation. It effectively communicated the problem, the unique solution, market validation, and the company's vision. This helped them raise $600,000, setting the stage for their subsequent success.

In the end, your pitch deck needs to tell a compelling story about your business—where it stands, where it's headed, and how it plans to get there. And always remember, simplicity and clarity go a long way in winning over potential investors.

Pitch Decks Gone Wrong

A pitch deck is a vital tool for an entrepreneur, outlining the business model, value proposition, ideal customer profile (ICP), market analysis, and go-to-market strategy for potential investors. However, crafting a pitch deck that hits the mark can be a steep learning curve for many, particularly for academic entrepreneurs who, while they may be experts in their field, can fall prey to the curse of knowledge we've already touched on above.

A classic example comes to mind. A group of researchers pitching a promising nanotechnology venture arrived armed with an overwhelming 100-slide presentation. While their technology was groundbreaking, they got so wrapped up in the scientific details that they lost sight of the bigger picture and how this would turn into a real market-beating product. Their pitch turned into a dense, data-heavy lecture filled with scientific terms and diagrams. The investors, though impressed with the technology, were left grappling with the core market application, the potential return on investment, and, crucially, why they should believe that this is investment ready. The aftermath was unfortunately predictable; the team didn't hear back from the "money people."

The problem was not in the technology itself but in the communication. The team failed to make their complex ideas accessible and relatable to their audience. The art of the pitch lies in balancing technical details with the bigger picture—clarifying the problem that the product solves, identifying the market gap it fills, and outlining the plan for growth and return on investment.

So, here are some of the many critical mistakes I have witnessed that can sink a venture's chances:

- Vague value proposition: Failing to clearly articulate what unique value your startup provides makes it hard for investors to grasp why your business will succeed. Avoid generic claims and industry jargon.

- No demonstration of market traction: Investors want to see evidence that people actually want your product. Lack of customer testimonials, revenue growth metrics, or partnerships is a red flag.

- Unclear target customer: If you can't clearly define who your customers are, investors will doubt you understand your market. Avoid hypothetical or overly broad customer profiles.

- Focusing too much on technology: Don't get bogged down in technical details. Focus on explaining the customer problem and your solution in simple terms.

- Spelling or grammatical errors: Typos and sloppy formatting undermine your credibility and leave a poor impression. Proofread extensively and have others review.

- Inconsistent branding: If your branding varies from slide to slide, it signals a lack of coordination and professionalism. Ensure uniformity in color schemes, logos etc.

- Information overload: Cramming too much text or data onto slides overwhelms your audience. Prioritize key data points and keep wording concise.

- Lack of visuals: Text-heavy slides with no graphics, charts or images are boring and hard to digest. Use visuals to tell your story better.

So, creating a compelling pitch deck is part science, part art form. While there is no set formula, avoiding these common pitfalls will help your presentation connect with investors and drive your fundraising success.

Guy Kawasaki, a well-known venture capitalist and author of *The Art of the Start 2.0*, advocates for a 10-slide pitch deck model. This model encourages entrepreneurs to be concise, clear, and focus on the crucial elements of the venture—problem, solution, business model, and GTM strategy. Remember, investors are not just interested in what your offering is. They are keen to understand its market fit, your strategy for market penetration and growth, and your traction to date. They want to see your understanding of the market and your plan to reach and engage ever more customers.

Consider structuring your pitch using the Pyramid Principle, a method developed by Barbara Minto at McKinsey & Company. The principle suggests starting with the main point (the problem you're solving, your unique solution, your market opportunity) and then providing supporting arguments and evidence. This top-down approach ensures the key message is delivered upfront, creating a strong, positive impression from the start without getting lost in the minutiae.

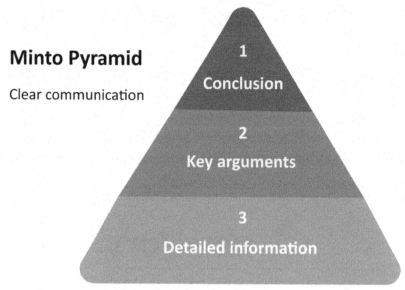

Minto Pyramid

Clear communication

1
Conclusion

2
Key arguments

3
Detailed information

(FIGURE 34: THE PINTO PYRAMID)

Successful examples of effective pitches abound. Airbnb's pitch deck began with a clear problem statement and their unique solution, followed by market validation. They demonstrated traction through customer and revenue growth. The deck ended with an overview of their business model, financials, and a clear ask from investors. This simple, clear, and direct approach helped Airbnb secure $600,000 in their seed round and springboarded their subsequent success.

In summary, academic entrepreneurs need to strike a balance in their pitch decks and follow a logic that allows the important strategic facets to be digested first. While it's important to explain the technology, it's crucial that you communicate its market potential in a language that resonates with potential investors. Only then will you stand a chance of securing the funding necessary for your new venture. The next chapter, explores another critical phase of your startup journey: how to scale.

But first, let's now conclude this chapter with a case study on Mapillary.

CASE STUDY: MAPILLARY

Mapillary, a Swedish startup, had a powerful vision: "We believe that everyone should have access to good maps." They coupled this grand vision with a unique offering—a crowdsourced, navigable street-level view of the world, quite similar to Google's Street View. The novel idea, driven by a blend of social good and technological innovation, had a significant appeal. But transforming this appeal into tangible investor interest needed a masterfully crafted pitch.

(FIGURE 35: MAPILLARY)

A standout feature of Mapillary's pitch was their effective use of structuring their narrative with a clear problem-solution approach, a method that echoes the key principles of the Pyramid Principle. This communication technique suggests starting with the main idea and then providing supporting arguments and evidence.

Their main idea revolved around a simple, powerful statement: the world needs better maps, and everyone should have access to them. This was followed by laying out the existing problem: despite the importance of digital mapping in modern life, many parts of the world were still unmapped or poorly mapped. Then came their unique solution: a platform that anyone with a smartphone could contribute to, making map-making a democratic, accessible process.

But what truly set them apart was their innovative edge. They showcased their advanced computer vision technology capable of automatically stitching together images and recognizing objects within them. This technical prowess made their crowdsourced solution not just feasible, but also scalable and efficient.

The company's pitch was a great example of clarity, simplicity, and vision. It was not just a showcase of their unique offering but a demonstration of their potential for achieving significant impact. They managed to highlight the value they brought to the table, their innovative solution to a global problem, and their potential for future growth. This compelling narrative, built around their vision and technology, successfully garnered investor interest, to mutual benefit.

Highlight: Mapillary's effective pitch played a critical role in their fundraising efforts, helping them secure multiple rounds of funding. Eventually, the strength of their product and the clarity of their vision led to their acquisition by Facebook in 2020, which demonstrated the potential of a well-structured, compelling pitch for attracting not only investment but also acquisition interest.

CHAPTER 15:
Financing Your Venture

Embarking on the startup journey often feels like learning a new language for many academics. This new vocabulary is laden with phrases such as *bootstrapping, venture capital*, and *private equity*, each representing different facets of the startup financing ecosystem that are entirely new to most academic founders. Navigating this challenge can be formidable; Understanding "the game" entails not only learning new terminology but a fundamental shift in mindset. As this chapter unfolds, we'll attempt to demystify these terms, and chart a course from bootstrapping to venture capital.

At the heart of this journey lies the process of financing your venture. This process is complex and largely determined by the stage, scale, and character of your business. Academic founders need to find their way through these diverse funding avenues, starting from the initial phase of bootstrapping to the more advanced stages of seeking venture capital.

Moreover, they often tap into government grants, a source of funding that can prove pivotal during the early stages of your startup.

Early Stage Financing: The Bootstrapping Prelude

When startups first come to life, they often do so by relying on "bootstrapping," a grassroots financing approach that taps into personal savings, draws contributions from friends and family, or leverages initial, albeit modest, customer revenue. This stage can feel a lot like tightrope walking without a safety net, thus it's frequently referred to as the realm of the three Fs: friends, family, and fools.

Bootstrapping promotes creativity born of constraints - without outside funding, startups must find clever solutions utilizing existing assets. This austerity distills business models down to their essence. When bootstrappers eventually pursue investment, their refined ventures resonate with investors who can see demonstrated traction and discipline. Having already validated their concepts, bootstrapped startups obtain funding like Series A at higher valuations, with less dilution of ownership. In forcing startups to hone their business models upfront, bootstrapping thus primes them for success when seeking needed capital.

As the startup grows and scaling evolves from a far-off idea into an urgent necessity, the need for external financing takes center stage. Suddenly, the startup's financing journey can feel like a thrilling episode straight out of popular shows like *Silicon Valley* in the U.S. or *Dragon's Den* in the UK, where entrepreneurs pitch their ambitious ideas hoping to land that game-changing investment.

Indeed, these television shows have helped demystify and dramatize the startup financing process, stirring the imagination of many would-be academics and entrepreneurs. I fondly recall watching episodes of *Dragon's Den* with my then-teenage daughter, eyes glued to the screen as entrepreneurs walked into the den, their dreams and years of hard work condensed into a few crucial minutes.

One particular pitch still stands out in my memory. The entrepreneurs proposed using neuroscience to combat obesity and diabetes. The novel idea? A head-worn device that employed cranial nerve stimulation to suppress appetite and encourage weight loss. It was as though they'd plucked a page from an Isaac Asimov novel.

Now, you'd think the investors might relegate such an idea to the realms of science fiction, but they didn't. They saw a firm scientific base and a market potentially as expansive as the problem they aimed to solve. The fusion of nifty science and exciting market potential resonated with them and led to a successful deal.

That pitch made quite an impression on both of us, particularly my daughter who was already intrigued by the workings of the human brain and regularly read the works of neuroscience scholars like Damasio, Gazzaniga, and Sapolsky.

While I wouldn't say that watching that episode was the eureka moment that guided my daughter towards a career in neuroscience—she was already knee-deep in neuroscience textbooks and fond of using our family dinners to debate cognitive theories—it certainly added an exciting dash of entrepreneurial spirit to her existing academic interests.

However, while these shows offer a dramatized snapshot into the world of startup financing, they merely represent a slice of a much broader, and more complex environment. The actual external funding ecosystem is an expansive tableau, composed of a myriad of funding avenues, each with unique attributes and implications. So, let's summarize the possible funding routes:

1. **Bootstrapping**: Bootstrapping is like the "Bear Grylls" of startup financing. It's about survival and resourcefulness, using personal savings, reinvesting initial profits, or calling on friends and family to fund the venture. This stage often involves more sweat than cash and is a test of the entrepreneur's grit, determination, and ability to convince others about the potential of their idea. It forces founders to spend wisely and distil the business model to its essence.

2. **Angel Investment**: Angel investors are the fairy godparents of the startup world. They're affluent individuals who provide early-stage funding, usually in exchange for a slice of the company. And they often offer more than money, contributing their industry insights, contacts, and mentorship to help the fledgling startup get its bearings.

3. **Accelerators and Incubators**: Accelerators and incubators are like the "training camps" of the startup ecosystem. They offer support to startups in the form of mentorship, office space, and sometimes even funding. The key difference? Incubators nurture startups over a longer period, helping to hatch the business. Accelerators, on

the other hand, aim to speed up the growth of existing businesses, helping them to fly higher, faster (Also, see Appendix E)

4. **Venture Capital (VC):** Venture Capitalists are like the "sharks" of the startup world— they are looking for potential breakout businesses where they can invest substantial funds in exchange for equity. This often comes with a seat on the board and a say in major decisions. VC funding is usually pursued when the startup is ready to scale rapidly and enter new markets.

5. **Private Equity (PE):** Private equity is like the "growth hormone" for more mature companies. Typically, PE firms invest in established businesses with stable cash flows, aiming to optimize operations, drive growth, and ultimately sell for a significant profit. The key difference from VC is that PE is more about improving an existing business rather than nurturing a new, high-growth potential startup.

The Role of Government Grants

Situated between the bootstrapping phase and the external financing stage, government grants play a pivotal role in early-stage funding, particularly when it comes to academic startups. Various government bodies worldwide offer grants specially designed for startups, such as the Small Business Innovation Research (SBIR) program in the U.S., Horizon 2020 in the European Union, or Innovate UK grants.

Horizon Europe is the European Union's flagship research and innovation funding program with a budget of €95.5 billion between 2021-2027. Horizon Europe contains multiple elements that can benefit startups, including the European Innovation Council (EIC) which provides early-stage grants and investment for breakthrough innovations. The EIC Accelerator offers grant funding paired with equity investment for startups to help bridge the commercialization gap. Additionally, European Research Council (ERC) grants support pioneering research projects, while Marie Skłodowska-Curie Actions focus on training and mobility programs for research talent.

Another key program for UK Universities is Innovate UK, the national innovation agency. Innovate UK offers initiatives like Smart Grants, which provide funding for R&D at innovative SMEs. It also administers Innovation Loans that supply debt financing to support bringing new products and services to market. By leveraging these major European grant programs strategically, academic startups can access capital to transform research into real-world impact.

So, government grants, while attractive for the capital they provide without diluting equity, can sometimes feel like trying to solve a complex Rubik's cube—one that requires as much time and effort as it does skill and patience. The process for these grants can be rigorous and labyrinthine, potentially diverting your focus and resources from crucial tasks such as customer discovery, product development, and refining your go-to-market strategy.

In the language of economics, this is known as opportunity cost; the concept that choosing one option invariably means sacrificing another. In the world of startups, this could mean the potential trade-off between time spent navigating the complexities of grant applications versus time spent directly nurturing your venture in other ways. This fundamental principle is something that even the most erudite academics may sometimes overlook when they step into the unfamiliar arena of entrepreneurship and business.

Moreover, while many grants are designed to encourage early-stage market validation, they do not absolve founders of the need to undertake the initial groundwork. This includes prototyping their product or service and garnering feedback from potential customers. Consider it as less of a "get out of jail free" card and more of a "level up" opportunity in your entrepreneurial journey.

Grants, when used strategically, can be a powerful lever to pull in your startup's financial plan.

They can catalyze product development, fortify scaling efforts, and augment credibility. However, they should not be viewed as the magic bullet for all your funding needs. They're more akin to a springboard that can propel you forward, rather than the rocket fuel needed for a full-throttle launch and growth. As a startup progresses, it invariably has to look beyond grants towards other sources of financing. This evolution leads us to an important moment in every founder's journey—stepping onto the stage (or into the boardroom) to present their brainchild to potential investors. And here's where the art of pitching takes center stage.

From Grant Applications to Investor Pitch Decks

As you move on from grant applications and gain exposure to the world of external financing, your startup's pitch deck becomes the beating heart of your fundraising efforts. Think of your pitch deck as the canvas on which you paint your startup's narrative. It is through this that you communicate your vision, business model, and go-to-market strategy to prospective investors—a rich and complex topic that we explore in more detail in Chapter 15.

Your GTM strategy emerges as a vital part of your story, demonstrating to investors not just the compelling features of your product or service, but how you plan to market and distribute it in ways that generate profitable revenue. This is where you highligh your understanding of the market, your unique selling proposition, and your customer acquisition, engagement, and retention strategies – all of which can considerably enhance your pitch's appeal.

As we will discuss in greater depth later, don't mistake quantity for quality. Your pitch is not a platform to boast about the intricacies of your science or backgound details you may yourself regard as fascinating, but to address the audience's critical, often non-technical, questions. Clear, compelling and memorable messaging is key.

In the ensuing chapters, we go deeper into financing options and discuss crafting a compelling pitch deck that integrates your GTM strategy effectively. These insights will aid in captivating investor interest and securing the necessary funds to fuel your growth.

But first, let's discuss how Grab, the Asian ride-hailing startup, illustrates how they effectively pitched their business to investors.

CASE STUDY: GRAB

Grab, the ride-hailing startup that became a super-app, began as a humble project between two Harvard Business School classmates in Malaysia. Founders Anthony Tan and Tan Hooi Ling noticed a market gap in their home country where public transportation was fragmented, unreliable, and in many cases, unsafe.

(FIGURE 36: GRAB RIDE SHARE)

The two founders, leveraging their business school network, initially raised $25,000 in seed money to start their venture. The concept of ride-hailing was still nascent in Southeast Asia, and the co-founders faced an uphill battle in convincing investors to fund their venture.

However, their persistent highly targeted pitch highlighting the massive market opportunity, their deep local knowledge, and their innovative solution to a widespread problem, paid off. They managed to secure $10 million in their Series A funding round from Vertex Ventures, a subsidiary of Temasek Holdings. This was a significant amount of funding for a Southeast Asian startup at the time, marking one of the earliest indications of Grab's future potential.

As the company grew, its pitching approach evolved from highlighting the market opportunity to showcasing its team's execution capabilities, strategic initiatives, and resilience in the face of fierce competition, including from global giant Uber. In later funding rounds, Grab secured billions in investment from prominent global investors, including SoftBank and Toyota.

In 2018, in a landmark deal, Grab acquired Uber's Southeast Asia operations, effectively winning the ride-hailing battle in the region. Today, Grab offers a suite of services including food delivery, digital payments, and even financial services.

CHAPTER 16:
Avoiding Funding Pitfalls

In the process of securing financing for your startup, it is essential to understand the potential drawbacks of different funding sources. Each form of financing—bootstrapping, angel investment, venture capital, and government grants—brings with it unique challenges and pitfalls that need to be carefully managed. This chapter will offer a closer look at these potential issues and provide guidance on how to navigate them effectively.

Bootstrapping: Balancing Growth and Resources

As argued in the previous Chapter, bootstrapping involves self-funding your venture, often relying on personal savings, early revenue, or contributions from friends and family.

Bootstrapping forces startups to be creative with limited resources—a constraint that distills business models down to their essence. While full control is retained, growth can be constrained without external funding. However, the fiscal discipline boosts efficiency, allowing startups to balance ambitions with realistic capital.

Prizing creativity over funding, bootstrappers must deftly juggle priorities and cash flow. This austerity prepares startups for future funding by demonstrating traction and resilience. However, bootstrapping risks missing mentorship, networking, and external validation. Overall, this scrappy approach allows synthesizing grand visions with grounded execution.

Angel Investment: Equity Dilution and Investor Expectations

Angel investors provide capital in exchange for equity in the company. While they bring in much-needed funding and often valuable advice and network connections, accepting angel investment means giving up a part of your company's ownership.

Equity dilution can impact your control over your business and reduce your share of the profits in the long run. Additionally, angel investors usually seek high return on their investment, which can create pressure to rapidly grow and scale, sometimes at the expense of a more sustainable, gradual growth strategy.

Venture Capital: Control Issues and High Growth Pressure

Venture capital can fuel significant growth for your startup, but it often comes with its own set of challenges. Like angel investors, VCs also acquire equity in your company, which can lead to control issues. Some VCs might exert influence over strategic decisions, sometimes leading to disagreements or conflict.

Moreover, VCs seek substantial returns on their investment, typically aiming for a successful exit via an IPO or acquisition. This expectation can create a high-pressure environment, with the focus shifting towards rapid growth and scale, possibly overlooking important factors like customer satisfaction or employee welfare.

Government Grants: Avoiding Over-Reliance

As discussed in the previous chapter, government grants provide valuable funding opportunities without diluting equity. However, these grants can also present potential pitfalls.

Applying for and managing grants can be a time-consuming process, potentially diverting focus from core business activities like product development and customer engagement. There's also a risk of becoming overly reliant on grant funding, which could distract startups from developing sustainable revenue streams and exploring other funding sources.

Moreover, grants typically do not cover the extensive costs associated with scaling a business. Over-reliance on any single funding source, including grants, could limit the development of broader funding skills, such as pitching to VCs or negotiating investment terms. It's here that other sources of support, such as incubators and accelerators, can play a crucial role.

Incubators and Accelerators: Speed vs. Control

Incubators and accelerators offer early-stage startups a unique value proposition. Beyond capital, they provide a plethora of resources, including mentorship, networking opportunities, and often, a dedicated workspace. The aim is to accelerate the development of these young companies, giving them a strong foundation to build upon.

Incubators typically offer a more flexible program focusing on nurturing startup development over a longer time frame. Accelerators, on the other hand, provide a more intensive, often cohort-based program, designed to expedite startup growth within a few months. As with the other forms of support, while these programs offer significant benefits, there are potential pitfalls that founders need to be wary of.

Time Pressure: In the case of accelerators, the pressure to develop and scale within a set timeframe can be intense. The need to deliver results quickly might push startups towards premature scaling or rushed product development, which may have negative consequences in the long run. On the other side of the spectrum, incubators, without strict timelines, may lead to a lack of urgency or a slower pace of progress.

Equity Trade-Off: Most of these programs require startups to give up a portion of their equity in exchange for the provided capital and resources. Founders must carefully consider whether this trade-off is worth it. While the resources and network can be invaluable, losing a significant stake in the company can impact the founders' control and their share of profits upon exit.

Mismatch of Expectations: Not all accelerator or incubator programs are created equal. The quality of mentors, the relevance of the curriculum, and the value of the network can vary. If these aspects don't align with the startup's needs or industry, the benefits might not outweigh the costs.

Over-reliance: Relying heavily on the support system provided by these programs can lead to a "bubble effect," where startups might struggle to operate independently post-program. Furthermore, easy access to resources might limit the development of necessary entrepreneurial skills such as resourcefulness and resilience.

To avoid these pitfalls, due diligence is key. Startups considering these programs should thoroughly research each one's offering, speak to alumni, and critically assess the value of the resources against the equity they're asked to give up. A well-chosen program can be a major springboard, accelerating a startup's path to market success. But founders must stay vigilant, ensuring they retain their entrepreneurial independence and control over their venture's direction.

While securing funding and support from accelerators and incubators is crucial for startups, it's equally important to be aware of and address the potential challenges each presents.

The key is diversification. Leveraging a mix of funding sources allows startups to benefit from the unique advantages of each while mitigating their potential pitfalls. This balanced approach sets the stage for sustained growth.

Of course, as we conclude this chapter it is important to remember that funding is just one piece of the puzzle. Even with the right amount of funding, your startup can still fail if you do not execute properly which is the subject of our next chapter.

But first, let's explore our case study on Neumann Labs,

CASE STUDY: NEUMANN LABS

Neumann Labs is a biotechnology startup based out of Munich, Germany, founded in 2021 with the goal of revolutionizing cancer diagnostics. The company sought to leverage advancements in bio-informatics and genomics to develop a novel method of early-stage cancer detection.

∩NEUMANNLABS
(FIGURE 37: NEUMANN LABS)

When it came time to secure funding, the founders of Neumann Labs faced a dilemma. Traditional funding routes such as venture capital (VC) were a viable option, but these often came with strings attached, such as relinquishing control and equity. The team wanted to maintain its independence, so it opted for an unconventional path: equity crowdfunding.

Equity crowdfunding is a platform-based approach to fundraising that allows companies to raise capital from a large number of individual investors. This type of funding has become increasingly popular in recent years, as it offers a number of advantages over traditional funding sources, such as VC and angel investors.

One of the key advantages of equity crowdfunding is that it allows companies to maintain control over their business. Unlike VC investors, who typically expect to play an active role in the company's management, equity crowdfunding investors are more passive and typically do not have any say in the company's operations.

Another advantage of equity crowdfunding is that it is more accessible to a wider range of companies. VC investors are typically selective in their investments and focus on companies that have a strong track record and a high potential for growth. Equity crowdfunding platforms, on the other hand, are open to a wider range of companies,

including early-stage startups and companies that may not be considered attractive by VC investors.

However, equity crowdfunding also comes with some challenges.
One of the biggest challenges is that it can be difficult to raise significant amounts of capital through this method. Equity crowdfunding
campaigns are typically limited to a certain amount of time and a
certain fundraising goal. If the company does not reach its goal within
the allotted time, the campaign is unsuccessful and the investors
are refunded.

Another challenge with equity crowdfunding is that it requires the
company to disclose its technology and business model to the public.
This can be a challenge for biotech startups, which often have proprietary technology that they need to keep confidential.

Despite these challenges, Neumann Labs' equity crowdfunding campaign was a success. The company raised €2 million from over 1,000
investors, securing their seed funding goal. This capital allowed the
team to advance their research, develop their prototype, and validate
their business model.

The success of Neumann Labs' crowdfunding campaign demonstrates that equity crowdfunding can be a viable funding option for
biotech startups, even though it is not typical. For Neumann Labs,
equity crowdfunding represented an innovative way to secure capital
while preserving their independence.

Relevant Insights

Neumann Labs' case study offers a number of relevant insights for biotech startups and other companies considering equity crowdfunding:

- Equity crowdfunding can be a viable option for companies
  that want to maintain control over their business and that
  may not be considered attractive by VC investors.

- Equity crowdfunding campaigns can be successful, but it is important to set realistic fundraising goals and to have a well-thought-out campaign strategy.

- Equity crowdfunding requires companies to disclose their technology and business model to the public. This can be a challenge for biotech startups, but it is important to be transparent with potential investors.

Highlight: Neumann Labs' crowdfunding success is a testament to the power of equity crowdfunding as a funding option for biotech start-ups. By carefully considering the pros and cons of different funding sources and by developing a well-thought-out campaign strategy, biotech startups can leverage equity crowdfunding to secure the capital they need to advance their research and development efforts.

CHAPTER 17:

Execution Excellence: Translating Strategy into Action

Entrepreneurship is a landscape rife with unanticipated twists and turns. While a strategy serves as your guiding compass, execution shapes the trajectory and pace of your startup—and often determines its fate. The heart of Execution Excellence lies in its ability to adeptly turn strategies into tangible actions, making full use of tools and solutions that illuminate the core components of your business model, such as market research, IP landscaping, and pricing models.

In Chapter 8, we introduced the go-to-market strategy as your startup's precise blueprint detailing the who, what, when, and why of its journey. Yet, without adept execution, even the most detailed roadmap remains static on paper. The true essence of a strategy is unlocked when it transitions from ideation to implementation.

Execution, however, isn't about rigidly tracing a pre-determined path. It's a dynamic process that demands synergy across various initiatives, keen responsiveness to market shifts, meticulous oversight, and a relentless commitment to customers. The key lies in maintaining a balance between being precise and adaptable, adhering to the planned course while leaving space for innovation and timely pivots.

In this chapter, we explore the intricacies of execution excellence, shedding light on how startups can breathe life into their strategies. We'll navigate the terrain of ensuring alignment across multiple initiatives, adapting to the ever-shifting marketplace, avoiding common pitfalls, and tracking progress. As we embark on this exploration, you'll discern that execution isn't a one-off event; it's a continuous interplay of precision, innovation, adaptability, and accountability.

As aptly put, "Strategy without execution is hallucination." A stellar strategy loses its luster without robust execution. In the sections that follow, we aim to unpack the complex world of execution, offering tangible insights and methods to realize your startup's goals.

Effectively executing a GTM strategy signifies the juncture where aspirations and reality converge. To transform strategic visions into tangible results, startups need an approach that resonates with their audience, aligns with their core values, and retains the agility to navigate the unpredictable business ecosystem. This chapter aims to guide you through the nuanced journey from strategic planning to execution, equipping you with the insights to turn your strategic ambitions into real-world triumphs.

Embarking on the path of execution excellence is about mastering the alchemy of transforming visions into realities. It encompasses the art of operationalizing strategies, fostering unity across teams, adapting to fluid business terrains, mitigating risks, and assessing outcomes. Through this journey, you'll recognize that execution is a harmonious blend of discipline, creativity, agility, and accountability, acting as the catalyst that converts ideas into tangible impacts.

As we chart the course of execution in subsequent sections, our objective is to demystify its processes, offering you actionable insights to translate your startup's vision into tangible outcomes.

Alignment and Adaptation

The bridge between strategy and execution is built on alignment and adaptation. This involves defining clear objectives and actionable tasks by setting SMART goals and breaking them down into achievable milestones. It also requires ensuring seamless communication and collaboration between different departments to achieve cross-functional alignment. Moreover, the importance of flexibility in responding to market shifts and unexpected challenges must be emphasized, which underlines the need for adapting to change.

A Customer-Centric Approach

Putting the customer at the heart of your execution ensures that your strategies resonate with the market. This approach entails understanding customer needs through continuous feedback and aligning offerings with customer expectations. Furthermore, it calls for enhancing the customer experience by engaging customers personally and ensuring quality at every touchpoint.

Measurement and Iteration

Execution is not a one-time event but an ongoing process of learning and growth. This section delves into defining and monitoring Key Performance Indicators (KPIs) by identifying critical success indicators and monitoring them regularly. It also encourages embracing failures as learning opportunities by viewing setbacks as chances to learn and improve. Finally, it stresses the importance of committing to continuous improvement, engaging in a cycle of continuous enhancement, always seeking opportunities to better efficiency, effectiveness, and customer satisfaction.

So, translating strategy into execution is both an art and a science, involving careful alignment, responsiveness to customers, and a commitment to continuous improvement. By understanding these key dimensions and integrating them into your execution process, you are positioning your startup for enduring success in a complex and competitive market.

Pumping the Revenue Engine:

While we have explored the intricate details of building an efficient and effective Revenue Engine in a previous chapter, it's crucial to reiterate its importance in the context of execution excellence. The Revenue Engine, encompassing marketing, sales, and customer success, is not just a theoretical concept but a dynamic system that requires careful orchestration. You need to ignite the engine, not just wait for it to rev up itself.

The Sales Process

The sales process is often where the rubber meets the road in translating strategy into revenue. We've previously covered the components of a successful sales strategy; now, let's focus on how this strategy becomes action.

- **Systematic Approach:** Leveraging a systematic sales process means translating sales strategies into step-by-step actions. It ensures consistency, accountability, and scalability. The linkage between the sales process and overall execution should be seamless, reflecting the strategic priorities and customer-centric approach of the venture.

- **Adaptation:** An effective sales process is never stagnant. It must adapt to market changes, customer feedback, and competitive pressures. This adaptability should be embedded within the broader execution framework, enabling quick responses to opportunities and threats.

- **Measurement and Improvement:** As with other aspects of execution, the sales process must be under constant evaluation. The use of sales metrics, aligned with broader business KPIs, ensures that the sales efforts are contributing effectively to overall business goals.

Revenue Engine Integration

The integration of marketing, sales, and customer success isn't just a strategic choice; it's an operational imperative. Ensuring that these functions are working synergistically, with aligned goals and coordinated activities, is a critical aspect of execution excellence.

- **Alignment Across Functions:** From lead generation to customer retention, the alignment across different functions of the Revenue Engine ensures a smooth and unified customer experience. This requires clear communication, shared objectives, and collaborative efforts among marketing, sales, and customer success teams.

- **Leveraging Technology and Tools:** The deployment of CRM systems, marketing automation tools, and customer success platforms, as previously mentioned, is not just about efficiency. It's about enabling a cohesive and responsive Revenue Engine that can drive sustainable growth.

So, execution excellence is akin to orchestrating a symphony, where various instruments (strategy, customer-centricity, alignment, adaptation, sales process, and Revenue Engine) must play in harmony. It's about ensuring that each part is tuned perfectly to the whole, creating a coherent and impactful performance.

By intertwining the principles of execution with the insights gained from developing the Revenue Engine and employing a systematic sales process, you've set the stage for a performance that resonates with your key audience—your customers. The challenge now is to conduct this symphony with skill, passion, and precision, turning strategic notes into a melody of success.

Looking ahead to our next chapter on scaling, it's worth noting that execution excellence is not an end but a beginning. Once you've translated your vision into reality, the path to scaling your venture presents its own set of challenges and opportunities, requiring you to leverage the principles of execution even more acutely.

But before we explore the subject of ways to amplify growth and scale the business, let's explore how the principles of execution excellence come to life at Salesforce.

CASE STUDY: SALESFORCE

Salesforce is a global leader in cloud-based customer relationship management (CRM) software. The company has been praised for its innovative products, customer-centric approach, and operational excellence.

(FIGURE 38: SALESFORCE)

One of the key factors behind Salesforce's success is its commitment to execution excellence. The company has a systematic sales process that is meticulously mapped to align with strategic objectives. This process has helped Salesforce to achieve several notable successes, including:

- Segmentation and personalization: Salesforce segments its markets by size, industry, and specific needs. This allows the company to engage with customers in a personalized way that resonates with their individual challenges.

- Integration with marketing and customer success: Salesforce's sales process is integrated with its marketing and customer success teams. This ensures that customers have a consistent experience throughout their journey with Salesforce.

- Account-based selling: Salesforce's sales teams focus on targeted accounts rather than generic markets. This ensures that the company's resources are focused on the most promising opportunities.

In addition to its systematic sales process, Salesforce is also known for its agility in responding to market dynamics. The company listens to customer feedback and adapts its offerings to meet real-world needs. Salesforce also responds quickly to competitive pressures and emerging market opportunities.

Salesforce also prioritizes continuous improvement. The company uses data-driven decision-making to track sales performance and monitor KPIs. Salesforce also applies agile methodologies across its organization, promoting adaptability, continuous learning, and incremental improvement.

Finally, Salesforce invests heavily in employee development. The company understands that execution excellence starts with people. By investing in training and development, Salesforce creates a culture of continuous growth.

Salesforce's success is a testament to its commitment to execution excellence. The company's systematic sales process, agility in responding to market dynamics, and prioritization of continuous improvement have helped it to achieve sustained growth and become a global leader in CRM software.

Highlights: Execution excellence is the bedrock of success for new ventures. This is achieved through a systematic sales process, driving revenue and meeting business goals. Especially in fluid markets, agility is key, ensuring a competitive edge but this can only come through a strong team that follows clearly defined processes. Investing in its development is not just beneficial—it's essential for sustained performance.

CHAPTER 18:

Scaling: Amplifying Growth

Once an academic startup has successfully launched and penetrated the market, the impending step often involves scaling. This pivotal phase transcends mere expansion; it's about amplifying your venture's impact to cater to burgeoning demand while enhancing its performance and efficiency to capture more value.

Crucially, scaling requires reevaluating your source of competitive advantage. What fueled initial success may not sustain growth at scale. Academic founders must have a solid grasp of their startup's differentiating strengths to guide strategic choices enabling scaled impact. This necessitates the creation and fine-tuning of a potent revenue engine that drives consistent growth.

In this chapter, we delve into the complexities of scaling, its associated challenges, and the crucial role of your go-to-market strategy and revenue generation in this process.

Scaling a company—whether it's a startup or a large corporation—is not fully understood and is even less frequently accomplished. According to McKinsey (2021), 80% of startups never reach critical scale, noting that at larger companies, the challenge is even greater. Only 10 percent of S&P 500 companies have managed to outpace the GDP growth for a continuous period of 30 years or more.

What distinguishes high-growth companies from their competition are a few distinct qualities, but one critical advantage is the capability to seamlessly integrate marketing and sales functions into an effective revenue engine.

Scaling, in its essence, is an economic principle rooted in the concept of "economies of scale." This kicks in when increasing production results in a decline in the cost per unit of output, enabling larger firms to produce goods or services more cost-effectively than their smaller rivals. In the context of a startup, it also implies building and refining the strategies that convert market presence into consistent revenue growth.

Consider a bakery as an illustration. Crafting a single loaf of bread incurs high costs, from rent and equipment (fixed costs) to ingredients and labor (variable costs). However, manufacturing 1,000 loaves distributes these fixed costs, thereby reducing the cost per loaf. This fundamental mechanism propels businesses to elevate their output and profits.

Although scaling can unlock substantial potential to boost profitability, it is fraught with risks. Accelerated growth can stretch your resources thin, disrupt operations, dilute your company culture, and potentially alienate customers if not adeptly managed. The challenge lies in skillfully navigating these growing pains while capitalizing on the vast opportunities that scaling creates.

Indeed, the risks associated with scaling can vary dramatically based on your business model as in the case of tech companies which might grapple with data privacy and security issues as they scale; or manufacturing firms that might encounter supply chain disruptions or environmental concerns. A case in point is the auto industry in Europe, which is facing an imminent ban on diesel-run cars, a trend that is likely to be followed by other regions.

Consider Spotify, the highly successful music streaming company. As Spotify's user base grew, its operating costs, especially music licensing fees, surged. This is because Spotify must pay a royalty to the copyright holders of each song that is streamed on its platform. As the number of users increases, so does the music that is streamed, and therefore the amount of royalties that Spotify must pay.

Spotify's experience demonstrates the scaling challenge of balancing growth with profitability. Music licensing fees are a variable cost, meaning that they increase as the number of users grows. This can put a strain on Spotify's profitability, especially in the early stages of growth.

Thus, scaling is a complex and multifaceted concept, requiring more than just escalating the volume of your products or services sold. It entails streamlining your business operations, broadening your value proposition, and adeptly managing growth-associated risks.

What is more, the process of scaling can differ significantly across industries and business models. Comprehending these nuances and strategically planning for them is crucial as you steer a scaling path forward.

Remember, scaling isn't just about expanding; it's about enhancing. It's about delivering more value to your customers, refining your operational efficiency, and catalyzing sustainable growth. It's about evolving from a promising venture to an industry leader.

As you gear up to scale, your GTM strategy remains a crucial lynchpin for successful expansion. An effective GTM strategy should be inherently scalable, and capable of accommodating escalating customer demand without a proportional increase in resources. As your venture gears up for scaling, it's essential to revisit your GTM strategy and finetune it as necessary.

Based on the study by global consulting firm McKinsey that reviewed over 200 scaled corporate startups, scaling demands an evolved approach compared to the initial market penetration phase. It identified 7 core-business scaling dimensions and 28 practices (such as solution delivery, usage tracking or feature build) that determine the success of scale-ups (McKinsey, 2022). They go on to argue that firms need to achieve at least a baseline competence in each of the following seven core business scaling dimensions:

1. **Product and Strategy:** This dimension involves having a product that meets the market needs and is scalable, and a strategy that aligns with the company's long-term objectives. It emphasizes the importance of the product and the overarching business strategy in the scaling process.

2. **Go-to-Market (GTM):** This pertains to the strategies and tactics a company uses to sell its products or services. It involves

understanding the customers, defining the value proposition, and aligning marketing, sales, and customer service to deliver this value effectively.

3. **Technology:** For scaling, the technology infrastructure should be robust and flexible enough to accommodate growth. It refers to the systems, applications, and platforms used in delivering products or services and how they can adapt to increased demand.

4. **People:** This dimension emphasizes the importance of hiring the right people, developing talent, and building a strong culture as the venture scales. It's about having a team that can support growth, and a culture that encourages innovation and agility.

5. **Operations:** Efficient and scalable operations, including production, delivery, customer service, and back-end processes, are crucial for scaling. It involves the daily activities and processes that produce and deliver the venture's products or services.

6. **Capital:** Scaling often requires significant resources. This dimension is about having a sound financial strategy, which includes securing the necessary funding, managing cash flow, and ensuring a good return on investment.

7. **Governance:** As ventures scale, they require more formal structures and processes to manage the increasing complexity. This dimension involves the systems and processes that ensure proper decision-making, accountability, and control.

Failure in even one practice within a dimension (say, solution delivery) will hinder a company's growth ambitions. Excelling in certain practices like product and strategy, GTM, technology, operations, capital, and governance can set apart the best performers. But it's important to remember that the practices that matter the most can vary based on the business itself.

As you seek a better understanding and ways to refine your strategy, it's essential that you distinguish between growth and scaling. While growth entails increasing both revenue and costs, scaling is about expanding your revenue exponentially with only a marginal rise in costs. A prime example of successful scaling is Google, which significantly grew its customer base with a minimal investment of resources, thereby boosting its profit margin in just a few years.

A formidable competitor to Google could have been Alibaba, the Chinese online search giant founded by Jack Ma. The company did very well, as it sought to leverage its huge domestic market and cultural relevance until the Chinese government severely curtailed its growth through stringent content controls. Alibaba's initial success was predicated on its deep understanding of the Chinese market and its ability to tailor its offerings to meet the needs of local consumers. However, the company's failure to anticipate and adapt to the changing regulatory landscape ultimately led to its downfall.

The key metrics that indicate your venture's health and success, such as gross margin, customer acquisition cost (CAC), lifetime value of a customer (LTV), and churn rate, become even more important in the context of scaling. For example, a healthy LTV to CAC ratio often signals a robust and scalable business model.

However, it's critical to remember that scaling is a milestone, not the destination. The ultimate goal is sustained growth, characterized by continuous expansion, innovation, increased market share, profitability, and customer satisfaction. And for all this, we'll need to calibrate our approach according to the culturally and regulatorily diverse global markets in which we operate.

As you seek a better understanding and ways to shape your strategy, it's essential that you distinguish between growth and scaling.

Scaling Models

When the time comes to scale, startups have several models to consider that align with their product, customers, and capabilities.

One option is the direct sales model which involves ramping up an internal sales team to connect with customers directly. Software company Salesforce scaled successfully using this model, rapidly expanding its salesforce to target large enterprises.

The channel sales model provides an alternative by leveraging indirect channels like resellers, distributors, and affiliates to expand reach. Computing giant Dell scaled up by selling its products through retail partners, allowing it to quickly gain consumer market share without building out its own retail presence.

Licensing core technology to capable partners is another pathway to commercializing innovation at scale. Biotechnology firm Genentech licensed out its groundbreaking recombinant DNA technology to other pharmaceutical firms, allowing its innovation to achieve widespread industry impact.

For businesses with a networked component such as ride-sharing platforms, the marketplace model can facilitate rapid growth by bringing large numbers of producers and consumers onto the platform. Transportation disruptor Uber scaled its business by getting drivers and riders in cities across the globe onto its platform.

Usage-based models centered on consumption rather than one-time sales can also serve as an engine of growth. Media streaming pioneer Netflix fueled its growth through a usage-based subscription model that gave consumers unlimited on-demand access rather than single purchases.

Evaluating these diverse scaling models and identifying examples of companies executing them successfully can help startups determine the optimal strategy to achieve ambitious growth goals.

The model that is best suited will depend on factors like the startup's product, target users, and internal capabilities.

Scaling with Local Knowledge

As your venture begins to mature and you're looking to scale, the critical importance of local knowledge becomes even more pronounced. The process of scaling involves expanding beyond your initial market or markets into new geographical areas, customer segments, or product lines. And with each new venture, the need to understand the local context and adapt accordingly cannot be overstated.

Often, startups think that they can apply the same strategies that worked in their initial market to new ones. But this assumption is very often flawed. What worked in one region might not work in another due to a myriad of factors such as cultural differences, diverging consumer preferences, varying regulatory frameworks, and disparate competitive dynamics.

The importance of local knowledge for scaling a business is especially evident in the Chinese electric vehicle (EV) market. Two leading Chinese EV manufacturers, BYD Auto and LI Auto, have successfully scaled their businesses by leveraging their deep understanding of the Chinese market and its unique challenges and opportunities.

BYD Auto, which had an early investor in Warren Buffett, has become one of the world's largest EV manufacturers by focusing on the development of affordable and reliable EVs for the Chinese market. The company has also benefited from government support for the EV industry in China.

LI Auto, which has a European distribution agreement with Lotus Cars, has also scaled its business successfully by understanding the needs of Chinese consumers. The company's flagship product, the Li ONE, is a plug-in hybrid SUV that is specifically designed for the Chinese market. The car offers a long range on electric power and a gasoline engine that can be used for extended trips.

The success of BYD Auto and LI Auto demonstrates the importance of local knowledge for scaling a business successfully. Startups that are looking to expand into new markets should carefully study the local market conditions and tailor their offerings to meet the needs of local consumers.

So, scaling is not merely about increasing the volume of your output or broadening your customer base, as I've already argued. Rather, it requires a nuanced and strategic approach to understanding and adapting to each new market you enter. Local knowledge can be gleaned through various methods, such as on-the-ground market research, hiring local experts, or collaborating with local partners. These can help make you more nimble and effective.

It's essential to note that localization is not a one-time process but an ongoing commitment. Market dynamics, consumer preferences, and regulatory controls are continually evolving, requiring businesses to keep their fingers on the pulse of local markets and adapt as needed.

Successfully scaling a business is no easy task, but with a deep understanding of local contexts and a commitment to adaptability, startups can maximize their chances of achieving sustained growth and prosperity.

For academic startups in particular, navigating the journey from lab to market involves surmounting numerous challenges and uncertainties. But with a clear understanding of your market and the myriad of local contexts, a meticulously crafted GTM strategy, and a readiness to adapt and learn, these challenges can transform into stepping stones to success.

CASE STUDY: SPOTIFY

Launched in 2006, the Swedish audio streaming pioneer Spotify revolutionized the music industry at a time when it was grappling with piracy issues and declining CD sales. Spotify's innovative model, offering access to millions of songs either for free (ad-supported) or through an ad-free monthly subscription, gained traction—the idea was great; the timing was right.

(FIGURE 39: SPOTIFY)

However, what set Spotify apart from competitors was its technological prowess and ability to scale. In the digital world, businesses like Spotify benefit from minimal marginal costs— the cost of serving an additional user is negligible which is a characteristic example of a digital technology.

Over time, Spotify expanded its reach globally, continuously introducing new features like playlists, podcast hosting, and social sharing capabilities. By 2021, Spotify boasted 345 million active users and had fundamentally transformed how people listen to music—not just millennials, but people in high age brackets.

Achieving such scaling wouldn't have been possible without the company's investment in technology infrastructure, data analytics, and a robust recommendation algorithm. By delivering personalized music experiences, Spotify has been able to increase the value delivered to each user, contributing to its long-term growth and customer retention.

Of course, the journey to scale wasn't without its challenges. As Spotify grew, so did its operating costs, particularly music licensing fees. This detail highlights an often overlooked complexity of scaling—although the cost of onboarding an additional user may be minimal, other costs, like music licensing fees, can increase substantially with growth.

Consequently, Spotify had to compete with tech giants like Apple and Amazon, who were leveraging their extensive resources, customer base, and ecosystems to promote their music streaming services. But Spotify's first-mover advantage, a dual revenue model (ad-supported free service and ad-free premium subscription), and focus on personalized music discovery served as unique selling propositions—and enabled it to stare down the competition.

In the face of these challenges, Spotify's successful scaling can be traced back to its proficiency in key dimensions of planning and execution—namely product and strategy, go-to-market, technology, and operations. So, the company's success serves as a powerful illustration of the importance of excelling across these dimensions which are critical to scaling successfully.

Highlights: Spotify's success is attributed to technological excellence, scalability, and continuous feature evolution. In the span of a few years, it catered to millions of active users across various age groups, globally. Despite challenges like rising operating costs and competition from tech giants, the company's unique selling propositions and proficiency in product strategy, market approach, technology, and operations have solidified its dominant competitive position.

CHAPTER 19:
Future Trends and the Sustainability Imperative

Looking ahead, two key trends will shape the environment for academic start-ups: an intensifying focus on environmental and social sustainability, and the disruptive rise of artificial intelligence.

The former refers to the need to develop businesses that are environmentally and socially responsible—and the growing demand for sustainable products and services. Businesses that can meet this demand will be well-positioned to succeed in the future. Indeed, academic startups can play a leading role in developing sustainable businesses, as they have access to cutting-edge research and can collaborate with experts in sustainability. For example, academic startups are developing new technologies to reduce pollution, conserve energy, and improve water efficiency. They are also developing new business models that are more sustainable, such as circular economy models and social enterprises.

The other major and equally significant force is the transformative impact of AI. Technology (particularly that which is powered by AI) is having a profound impact on the way that businesses operate. AI can be used to automate tasks, improve decision-making, and develop new products and services. This has the potential to create new opportunities for academic startups, as they can use AI to develop innovative solutions to real-world problems.

However, it is important to ensure that AI is used in a responsible way that does not harm society or the environment. For example, AI could be used to develop autonomous vehicles that are more efficient and safer than human-driven vehicles. However, it is also possible that AI could be used to develop autonomous weapons that could kill without human intervention.

It is therefore essential for academic startups to consider the ethical implications of using AI. They should develop AI systems that are transparent and accountable, and that are designed to promote social good.

There are a number of challenges that academic startups face when trying to develop sustainable businesses and these have been receiving close scrutiny. One challenge is that sustainability can be expensive. It can be costly to develop and implement sustainable practices, and this can be a barrier for startups that are already operating on a tight budget.

Another challenge is that sustainability can be complex. There are many different factors to consider when developing a sustainable business, and it can be difficult to get everything right.

Finally, pursuing sustainability can be risky. There is always the possibility that a business model focused on sustainability rather than short-term profits will not end up being financially viable. This risk of lower financial returns is something startups may not be willing to take on.

So, there is a need to rethink our prevailing models and take action accordingly. Indeed, despite the challenges, it is essential for universities to play a role in addressing the sustainability imperative. They have a responsibility to educate students about sustainability and to conduct research that can help to develop sustainable solutions.

Universities can also support academic startups that are developing sustainable businesses. This can be done by providing funding, mentorship, and access to resources. Joining forces in the context of a triple helix model makes eminent sense: universities, governments, and businesses can create a more sustainable future.

So, let us examine these two forces in more detail.

The Transformative Impact of Technology

Artificial intelligence (AI) is at the forefront of technological innovation, as discussed throughout this book. Intensifying efforts to commercialize AI research from academic labs lead to divergent outcomes; naturally, many innovations fail to achieve market viability, but some of those that manage to successfully traverse the chasm become integral to our daily lives. They become part of the fabric of human existence."

In his insightful book *AI Superpowers: China, Silicon Valley, and the New World Order*, Kai-Fu Lee proposes that AI technologies, particularly generative AI, carry immense potential to reshape the startup ecosystem (Lee, 2018). Advanced generative AI models like OpenAI's GPT-4 or Google's Bard, initially sent ripples across fields as diverse as content creation, customer service, data analysis, and software development. These ripples have grown into waves that may soon turn into tsunamis of transformative change. The genie is out of the bottle. There is no turning back.

(FIGURE 40: CHATGPT)

Indeed, these sophisticated models have progressed beyond simple text generation, producing authentic, human-esque content in response to the prompts they're given. When integrated with plugins like Wolfram Alpha, which offers real-time computational capabilities and real-time data, they deliver enhanced, context-sensitive output, fueling the expansion of an AI-centric ecosystem.

Such technological advancements offer startups, especially those operating on a shoestring budget, an unprecedented opportunity to amplify their capabilities. As argued in earlier chapters, integrating AI systems into their operations enables startups to enhance efficiency, stimulate creativity, and fuel innovation - the key ingredients for gaining a competitive edge

I've already discussed at length the work of experts like Yuval Noah Harari and Nick Bostrom, both of whom emphasize AI's dual potential for progress and peril. They underscore AI's potential to reshape industries and society, while also highlighting risks like job displacement and existential threats if development outpaces governance. As I've argued time and again, managing these risks is imperative as AI becomes further embedded not just in our work but our very lives

The Sustainability Imperative

As we reflect on technology's profound influence, it's crucial to address the 'sustainability imperative' in academic entrepreneurship: the importance of nurturing businesses attuned to environmental and social responsibility, not just short-term profits. This is undoubtedly difficult given the prevailing focus on rapid growth and market forces that shape today's economy

Academic startups, with their access to cutting-edge research and sustainability experts, are at the forefront of this movement. They're pioneering technologies to tackle pollution, champion energy conservation, and optimize water use. Additionally, they are reimagining business paradigms, helping craft alternative models like circular economies and social enterprises.

A slew of alternative entrepreneurship models have emerged to address these challenges:

- **Social Enterprises**: Focused on addressing societal issues, they often reinvest profits back into the community or business.

- **Impact Investing**: Investors channel funds into businesses solving environmental or societal challenges, blending financial returns with positive impact.

- **Community-Based Entrepreneurship**: Prioritizing local community upliftment, this model collaborates with local entities to forge sustainable ventures.

With varied challenges and goals, the academic entrepreneurship ecosystem is likely to witness an expanded array of diverse models, tailored to specific contexts.

The Future of Work: Melding Sustainability & Efficiency

Academic startups aren't just grappling with sustainability; they're navigating the profound shifts reshaping work, propelled by disruptive forces like AI and digitalization. This digital transformation brings a double-edged sword: while it paves the way for innovation and global collaboration, it also mandates startups to be nimble, adaptable, and efficient.

To stay ahead, academic startups can intertwine efficiency with sustainability. For instance, remote work can reduce carbon footprints linked to commutes and office upkeep. Digital collaboration tools can supplant business travel, further shrinking environmental impact.

In my lectures and writings, I've emphasized the changing nature of "jobs" and its implications for how we manage. As I've already argued, the future lies in disassembling job roles, modularizing tasks, and reassembling them in configurations that embrace efficiency and eco-consciousness. We can then fluidly redeploy resources, and integrate diverse expertise, while demonstrating a commitment to sustainable values.

In this dynamic arena, academic startups must evolve with agility and foresight. We can do this by merging contemporary work modalities with eco-principles while maximizing efficiency and maintaining adaptability. This isn't just strategic—it's an existential necessity. As we forge ahead, our success hinges on a potent blend of innovation, resilience, adaptability, and staunch dedication to sustainability principles.

Now let's examine the case of BenevolentAI which exemplifies the transformative impact of AI and how sustainability objectives have been woven into the company's strategy.

CASE STUDY: BENEVOLENTAI

BenevolentAI is a global leader in using AI to accelerate drug discovery and development. The company's mission is to elevate patient care and deepen our understanding of diseases through the innovative application of AI in biomedical research. BenevolentAI's AI platform is able to analyze vast amounts of biomedical data to identify patterns and connections much quicker and more accurately than conventional methods. This capability allows the company to significantly shorten the drug discovery timeline and reduce associated costs.

(FIGURE 41: BENEVOLENTAI)

In addition to its focus on drug discovery, BenevolentAI is also committed to using its technology to address global health challenges and reduce the environmental impact of drug development. The company's sustainability objectives are reflected in its corporate culture and practices.

For example, BenevolentAI has a strong commitment to diversity and inclusion. The company's workforce is made up of people from all over the world with a variety of backgrounds and experiences. This diversity of perspectives is essential for innovation and creativity.

BenevolentAI is also working to reduce its environmental impact by offsetting its carbon emissions. The company also uses sustainable practices in its operations, such as recycling and energy conservation.

Here are some specific examples of how BenevolentAI is using its technology to promote sustainability:

- Developing new drugs to treat diseases that are caused by environmental factors, such as air pollution and climate change.

- Working to reduce the use of animal testing in drug development.

- Developing more efficient and sustainable manufacturing processes for drugs.

BenevolentAI's commitment to sustainability is commendable and sets a good example for other academic startups. The company's success demonstrates that it is possible to use AI to improve healthcare while also reducing the environmental impact of the pharmaceutical industry.

Highlight: BenevolentAI is a leading example of how AI can be used to improve healthcare and promote sustainability. The company's commitment to diversity and inclusion, as well as its efforts to reduce its environmental impact, are commendable and set a good example for other academic startups.

EPILOGUE:
Charting a Course Forward

In this book, we have explored the realm of academic startups, a fascinating intersection where pioneering research converges with the vibrant yet uncertain world of entrepreneurship. The allure of these startups is rooted in the transformative technologies they champion. Yet, absent a solid go-to-market (GTM) strategy, even the most promising of these ventures risk falling short, failing to harness their potential—a potential that, if unleashed, has the power to redefine our everyday lives.

Traversing through the challenges these startups face, especially the dreaded "valley of death," has underlined the imperative nature of adaptability, resilience, and a relentless pursuit of knowledge. It's a quest, where not just the innovation, but the journey itself offers a treasure trove of learning experiences.

Our exploration underscores a striking observation: the literature on academic entrepreneurship has burgeoned over the years, reflecting its increasing significance in the modern world. This surge of interest isn't mere academic curiosity. The generation of wealth from research activities stands at an intersection of huge importance and increasing sensitivity, especially given today's pressing sustainability challenges.

Advances in fields like artificial intelligence and quantum computing present promising opportunities for academic startups to develop innovative solutions to pressing societal challenges. These technologies could enable startups to make breakthroughs that transcend academia and business. However, the trajectory of such startups is multifaceted, influenced by myriad variables beyond the technology itself. A closer look reveals systemic features, as academia's venture into entrepreneurship represents a confluence of technology, market dynamics, socio-economic currents, and sustainability goals.

At the nucleus of these endeavors stand the founders and their teams. These scholars, stepping out from the comfortable cocoon of academia, are the torchbearers who not only innovate but are also driven by an ethos of exploration combined with responsibility. They exemplify a new breed of entrepreneurs focused not just on profitability but on creating a lasting societal impact, addressing not only our generation's challenges but those of the future.

Academia serves as a crucible of innovation, producing the groundbreaking research that has the potential to revolutionize industries and societies. However, there is often a chasm between the raw materials that academia delivers and the tools and language necessary to convert this potential into tangible market offerings. Translating intricate research into a viable business proposition demands a distinct lexicon, one that persuades and resonates in the bustling corridors of commerce. This intricate dance of translation is a challenge I have endeavored to confront since getting involved in the world of academic startups.

As they stand on the cusp of rewriting conventional business practices, these startups are champions of dual innovation. On one hand, they break boundaries in the domain of technology, and on the other, they are pioneers of sustainable business models. This ensures their undertakings are not only commercially viable but are also addressing pressing societal challenges.

At the heart of it all lies a fundamental principle: while tried and tested GTM strategies offer invaluable blueprints, the true essence of success is the ability to mold these frameworks to fit unique contexts. There is no universal formula, no magic bullet. It is the harmonious integration of academic rigor, an entrepreneurial spark, and the agility to navigate ever-evolving contexts that steers the ship forward.

To all founders, pioneers, and risk-takers embarking on this voyage, may your journey be one of exploration, innovation, and lasting impact. As we close this chapter, always bear in mind that the triumph of any GTM strategy is deeply rooted in its adaptability to myriad contexts. In the realm of academic startups, we don't seek a one-size-fits-all solution but a diverse arsenal of strategies, each tailored to distinct needs, markets, and aspirations. With that, I raise a toast to the unwritten, yet promising, future!

REFERENCES

Anderson, C. (2012). *Makers: The New Industrial Revolution*. Crown Business.

Auerswald, P. E. (2015). *The Code Economy: A Forty-Thousand Year History*. Oxford University Press.

Birkinshaw, J. (2012). *Making Sense of Ambidexterity*. *INSEAD*.

Blank, S., & Dorf, B. (2012). *The Startup Owner's Manual: The Step-By-Step Guide for Building a Great Company*. K&S Ranch.

Bostrom, N. (2014). *Superintelligence: Paths, Dangers, Strategies*. Oxford University Press.

Bourdieu, P., & Passeron, J. C. (1990). *Reproduction in Education, Society and Culture*. Sage.

Brin, S., & Page, L. (1998). The anatomy of a large-scale hypertextual Web search engine. *Computer Networks and ISDN Systems, 30*(1-7), 107-117.

Brown, C. G., Clarke, J., & Warwick, R. (2021). Oxford Nanopore sequencing in microgravity. *NPJ Microgravity, 3*, 5.

Burgelman, R. A. (1991). Intraorganizational ecology of strategy making and organizational adaptation: Theory and field research. *Organization Science, 2*(3), 239-262.

Burgelman, R. A., & Grove, A. S. (2007). Let Chaos Reign, Then Rein In Chaos - Repeatedly: Managing Strategic Dynamics For Corporate Longevity. *Strategic Management Journal, 28*(10), 965-979.

Bower, J. L., & Christensen, C. M. (1995). Disruptive Technologies: Catching the Wave. *Harvard Business Review, 73*(1), 43-53.

Christensen, C. M., & Raynor, M. E. (2003). Why Hard-Nosed Executives Should Care About Management Theory. *Harvard Business Review, 81*(9), 66-74.

Christensen, C. M., Kaufman, S. P., & Shih, W. C. (2008). Innovation Killers: How Financial Tools Destroy Your Capacity to Do New Things. *Harvard Business Review, 86*(1), 98-105.

Clark, B. R. (1998). *Creating Entrepreneurial Universities: Organizational Pathways of Transformation.* Pergamon.

Combs, J. G., Ketchen, D. J. Jr., Terjesen, S. A., & Bergh, D. D. (2023). After the startup: A collection to spur research about entrepreneurial growth. *Strategic Entrepreneurship Journal.* August 2023.

Drucker, P. (1985). *Innovation and Entrepreneurship.* HarperCollins Publishers.

Drucker, P. (1985). The Discipline of Innovation. *Harvard Business Review, 63*(3), 67-72.

Druilhe, C., & Garnsey, E. (2004). Do academic spin-outs differ and does it matter? *Journal of Technology Transfer, 29*(3-4), 269-285.

Ehrenberg, A. (2020). *The Mechanics of Passion: Brain, Behaviour, and Society.* McGill-Queen's University Press.

Eisenhardt, K. M., & Martin, J. A. (2000). Dynamic capabilities: what are they? *Strategic Management Journal, 21*(10-11), 1105-1121.

Etzkowitz, H. (2003). Research groups as 'quasi-firms': the invention of the entrepreneurial university. *Research Policy, 32*(1), 109-121.

Fromm, E. (1963). *The Sane Society.* Routledge and Kegan Paul.

Geiger, R. L. (2002). *The American Research University from World War II to World Wide Web: Governments, the Private Sector, and the Emerging Meta-University.* University of California Press.

Godin, S. (2018). *This is Marketing: You Can't Be Seen Until You Learn to See.* Portfolio/Penguin.

Gompers, P., & Lerner, J. (2001). *The Money of Invention: How Venture Capital Creates New Wealth.* Harvard Business Press.

Hall, B. H., & Ziedonis, R. H. (2001). The patent paradox revisited: an empirical study of patenting in the US semiconductor industry, 1979-1995. *RAND Journal of Economics, 32*(1), 101-128.

Harari, Y. N. (2018). *21 Lessons for the 21st Century.* Spiegel & Grau.

Hsu, D. H., & Ziedonis, R. H. (2013). Resources as dual sources of advantage: Implications for valuing entrepreneurial-firm patents. *Strategic Management Journal, 34*(7), 761-781.

Jain, S., George, G., & Maltarich, M. (2009). Academics or entrepreneurs? Investigating role identity modification of university scientists involved in commercialization activity. *Research Policy, 38*(6), 922-935.

Jenkins, M., & Pasternack, B. A. (2014). *The Art of Strategic Leadership: How to Guide Teams, Create Value, and Apply Techniques to Shape the Future.* Wiley.

Lam, A. (2010). From 'ivory tower traditionalists' to 'entrepreneurial scientists'?: academic scientists in fuzzy university—industry boundaries. *Social Studies of Science, 40*(2), 307-340.

Levy, S. (2011). *In The Plex: How Google Thinks, Works, and Shapes Our Lives.* Simon and Schuster.

Loman, N., & Pallen, M. (2015). Twenty years of bacterial genome sequencing. *Nature Reviews Microbiology, 13*(12), 787-794.

Martin, R., & Lafley, A.G. (2013). *Playing to Win: How Strategy Really Works.* Harvard Business Review Press.

Maurya, A. (2012). *Running Lean: Iterate from Plan A to a Plan That Works* (2nd ed.). O'Reilly Media.

McKinsey Quarterly. (2021). How good are you at business building? A new way to score your ability to scale new ventures. *McKinsey Quarterly.*

McDonald, M., & Wilson, H. (2016). *Marketing Plans: How to Prepare Them, How to Use Them.* John Wiley & Sons.

Moore, G. A. (2014). *Crossing the Chasm: Marketing and Selling High-Tech Products to Mainstream Customers* (3rd ed.). HarperBusiness.

Morin, R. (2014). Why Are Some Academic Papers More Cited Than Others? The Influence of Author Reputation, Journal Reputation and Paper Length on Citations Received. *SAGE Open, 4*(1), 2158244014522637.

Mowery, D. C., Nelson, R. R., Sampat, B. N., & Ziedonis, A. A. (2001). The growth of patenting and licensing by U.S. universities: an assessment of the effects of the Bayh-Dole act of 1980. *Research Policy, 30*(1), 99-119.

Najmaei Lonbani, A. (2018). Architecture of Technology Ventures: A Business Model Perspective. In A. Presse & O. Terzidis (Eds.), *Technology Entrepreneurship: Insights In New Technology-Based Firms, Research Spin-Offs And Corporate Environments* (pp. 21-48). Springer.

North, D. C. (1991). *Institutions, Institutional Change and Economic Performance.* Cambridge University Press.

Olsen, D. (2015). *The Lean Product Playbook: How to Innovate with Minimum Viable Products and Rapid Customer Feedback.* Wiley.

Osterwalder, A., & Pigneur, Y. (2010). *Business Model Generation: A Handbook for Visionaries, Game Changers, and Challengers.* John Wiley & Sons.

Park, W. G. (2008). International patent protection: 1960–2005. *Research Policy, 37*(4), 761-766.

Pisano, G. P., & Verganti, R. (2008). Which kind of collaboration is right for you? *Harvard Business Review, 86*(12), 78-86.

Ries, E. (2011). *The Lean Startup: How Today's Entrepreneurs Use Continuous Innovation to Create Radically Successful Businesses.* Crown Business.

Ries, A., & Trout, J. (1981). *Positioning: The Battle for Your Mind.* McGraw-Hill.

Roberts, E. B., & Eesley, C. E. (2011). Entrepreneurial Impact: The Role of MIT. *Foundations and Trends in Entrepreneurship, 7*(1-2), 1-149.

Rosenberg, N., & Birdzell, L. E. (1986). *How the West Grew Rich: The Economic Transformation of the Industrial World.* Basic Books.

Rossides, N. (2023). *Engaging the Workforce: The Grand Management Challenge of the 21st Century.* Routledge.

Schumpeter, J. A. (1942). *Capitalism, Socialism and Democracy.* Harper & Brothers.

Shane, S. (2004). *Academic Entrepreneurship: University Spinoffs and Wealth Creation.* Edward Elgar Publishing.

Snow, C. P. (1959). *The Two Cultures.* Cambridge University Press.

Smith, M. L., & Seward, C. (2009). The relational ontology of Amartya Sen's Capability Approach: Incorporating social and individual causes. *Journal of Human Development and Capabilities, 10*(2), 213-235.

Teece, D. J. (2010). Business Models, Business Strategy and Innovation. *Long Range Planning, 43*(2-3), 172-194.

Teece, D. J., Pisano, G., & Shuen, A. (1997). Dynamic capabilities and strategic management. *Strategic Management Journal, 18*(7), 509-533.

Taleb, N. N. (2012). *Antifragile: Things That Gain from Disorder.* Random House.

Von Hippel, E. (2005). Democratizing innovation: The evolving phenomenon of user innovation. *Journal für Betriebswirtschaft, 55*(1), 63-78.

Zenger, T. R. (1992). Why Do Employers Only Reward Extreme Performance? Examining the Relationships Among Performance, Pay, and Turnover. *Administrative Science Quarterly, 37*(2), 198-219.

Zook, C., & Allen, J. (2016). *The Founder's Mentality: How to Overcome the Predictable Crises of Growth.* Harvard Business Review Press.

Zucker, L. G., Darby, M. R., & Armstrong, J. S. (2002). Commercializing knowledge: University science, knowledge capture, and firm performance in biotechnology. *Management Science, 48*(1), 138-153.

APPENDIX A:
Go-to-Market Strategy Checklist

A Go-to-Market (GTM) strategy is pivotal in determining how a venture will introduce its offerings to its target audience. For startups rooted in academia, this strategy bridges the gap between academic research and real-world market needs. It requires a balance of rigor and flexibility.

Key Steps in Developing a GTM Strategy:

1. **Understand the Market:** Immerse yourself in your target market. Understand your potential customers, assess competitors, and familiarize yourself with regulations specific to your academic sector.

2. **Define Your ICP (Ideal Customer Profile):** Sketch a detailed profile capturing the characteristics, needs, and behaviors of your optimal customer.

3. **Craft a Unique Value Proposition:** Highlight the distinct benefits your product/service brings to the fore for your target audience.

4. **Choose Your Market Entry Strategy:** Decide on the best approach to launch. Whether through direct sales, academic partnerships, IP licensing, or strategic alliances, your choice should mirror your startup's strengths and the market's dynamics.

5. **Formulate a Marketing Strategy:** Design campaigns to build awareness. Opt for channels that resonate with both the academic community and potential industry adopters.

6. **Design a Sales Blueprint:** Have a clear strategy for translating market interest into tangible sales or collaborations.

7. **Set Metrics and Monitor Them:** Pinpoint KPIs that reflect your GTM's effectiveness and ensure regular reviews.

Questions to Ponder:

- **Venture Capital Funding:** If your innovation demands significant investment, consider when to seek venture capital to bolster your GTM efforts.

- **Intellectual Property:** Protect your innovation. Familiarize yourself with patents, copyrights, and trademarks to ensure your research remains safeguarded.

- **Commercialization Path:** Understand whether licensing, establishing an independent venture, or direct sales aligns best with your offering and market appetite.

- **Networking:** Forge ties with fellow academic entrepreneurs, prospective backers, and industry experts. Such connections can substantially expedite your GTM journey.

- **Consistency in Branding:** Maintain a uniform brand voice and imagery across all touchpoints to foster brand recognition and credibility.

Ready-to-Use Checklist:

- ☐ Market insights secured?
- ☐ ICP detailed and ready?
- ☐ Value proposition articulated?
- ☐ Market entry strategy chosen?
- ☐ Marketing strategy set?
- ☐ Sales strategy charted?
- ☐ KPI tracking mechanisms in place?

Sales Strategy Options to Explore:

1. **Direct Sales Model:** Direct customer outreach.

2. **Inside Sales Model:** Digital or telephonic sales.

3. **Channel Sales Model:** Leverage resellers, affiliates, or distributors.

4. **Retail Sales Model:** Opt for brick-and-mortar outlets.

5. **Online Sales Model:** Utilize e-commerce platforms.

6. **Freemium Model:** Offer basic features for free with paid upgrades.

7. **Partnership Model:** Co-sell or bundle products with strategic allies.

8. **Wholesale Model:** Target retailers who then cater to end customers.

This checklist is a starting point. Each academic startup's GTM strategy will possess unique facets influenced by specific research nuances and market shifts. Always be adaptive and attuned to evolving demands.

APPENDIX B:

Key Performance Indicators (KPIs)

Startups thrive on metrics. They provide a clear picture of where the business stands and where it needs to go. Here's a condensed overview of some essential KPIs for startups:

Financial KPIs

- Revenue
  - ☐ Monthly recurring revenue (MRR)
  - ☐ Annual recurring revenue (ARR)
  - ☐ Total contract value (TCV)
  - ☐ Renewal rate
  - ☐ Net revenue retention (NRR)

- Gross profit
  - ☐ Gross margin
  - ☐ Cost of goods sold (COGS)
  - ☐ Gross profit margin

- Net income
  - ☐ Operating profit
  - ☐ Net profit margin
  - ☐ EBITDA (earnings before interest, taxes, depreciation, and amortization)

- Cash flow from operations
    - ☐ Free cash flow
    - ☐ Burn rate
    - ☐ Runway

- TAM (Total Addressable Market)
    - ☐ Market size
    - ☐ Market share
    - ☐ Market growth rate

Customer KPIs

- CAC (Customer Acquisition Cost)
    - ☐ Cost per lead
    - ☐ Cost per acquisition (CPA)
    - ☐ Customer acquisition efficiency (CAE)

- LTV (Lifetime Value)
    - ☐ Average customer lifetime value (ACV)
    - ☐ Customer lifetime value (CLTV)
    - ☐ Customer lifetime value churn (CLTVchurn)

- Churn rate
    - ☐ Monthly churn rate
    - ☐ Annual churn rate
    - ☐ Customer churn rate by cohort

- NPS (Net Promoter Score)
    - ☐ Promoter score
    - ☐ Detractor score
    - ☐ Passive score

- Customer satisfaction score
    - ☐ CSAT score
    - ☐ NPS score
    - ☐ Customer effort score (CES)

- Customer engagement
    - ☐ DAU (daily active users)
    - ☐ MAU (monthly active users)
    - ☐ WAU (weekly active users)
    - ☐ Session length
    - ☐ Page views per session

Operational KPIs

- Development time
    - ☐ Time to market
    - ☐ Time to launch
    - ☐ Time to feature

- Customer support response time
    - ☐ First response time
    - ☐ Resolution time
    - ☐ Customer satisfaction with customer support

- Marketing conversion rate
    - ☐ Landing page conversion rate
    - ☐ Email conversion rate
    - ☐ Social media conversion rate

- Employee engagement score
    - ☐ Employee engagement score
    - ☐ Employee satisfaction with their work
    - ☐ Employee turnover rate

- Onboarding success rate
    - ☐ Time to productivity
    - ☐ Percentage of new employees who are successful in their first 90 days

APPENDIX C:
Go-To-Market Toolkit

In Chapter 8, we ventured into the details of crafting robust GTM strategies and discussed the relevant tools in the chapter that follows. As we outline available toolkits in this appendix, special attention is paid to the transformative potential of AI, underscoring its game-changing impact on contemporary startups.

Innovation Assessment

The European Commission's initiative, the Innovation Radar, helps identify groundbreaking research and pioneering innovators. At its core, this platform offers an extensive database, richly embedded with myriad innovations from diverse sectors. This vast reservoir is not merely a compilation; it's a curated landscape, wherein each innovation is meticulously evaluated and categorized.

This meticulousness is evident as the platform evaluates innovations based on criteria such as market potential, technological maturity, innovator commitment, and proficiency in innovation management. As a result, each innovation is labeled with a unique "radar" classification, lucidly delineating its development stage and indicating its proximity to market readiness.

With the infusion of AI capabilities, the Innovation Radar's potential magnifies exponentially. It becomes more than a repository—it morphs into a predictive tool. Through sophisticated algorithmic analyses, it offers startups a gaze into the future. They can discern which innovations might become market sensations or pinpoint sectors primed for explosive growth in the upcoming years. This predictive prowess empowers startups with the foresight to strategically align their efforts in anticipation of these imminent market shifts, granting them an unparalleled competitive edge.

But the scope of the Innovation Radar doesn't end with future predictions. Its present value is undeniable. Startups, investors, and innovators can harness this tool to unearth exploitable results, zero in on potential partners, and, importantly, gain a deep understanding of the EU-funded innovation landscape. This not only provides clarity on current market conditions but also uncovers a plethora of opportunities ripe for exploration.

As this tool constantly evolves, reflecting the dynamism of the innovation ecosystem, it's prudent for users to stay updated with the most recent information directly from the EU Innovation Radar's official resources, ensuring they leverage the platform's full potential. In essence, the Innovation Radar, with its blend of exhaustive current data and AI-driven predictive capabilities, is an indispensable asset for any startup or innovator aspiring to thrive in today's complex, ever-evolving market landscape.

AI-driven Social Listening Platforms

The advent of AI has ushered in a new era for market research. Traditional tools, while valuable, often present data in a broad, aggregated form. But platforms like DMR and Crimson Hexagon are rewriting this script by leveraging the transformative potential of AI, offering startups precise, real-time, and deeply insightful analytics.

DMR employs advanced algorithms to analyze oceans of digital data, as we've already discussed in Chapter 9. These algorithms detect patterns, track real-time sentiment shifts, and even forecast potential market disruptions. A distinguishing feature of DMR is its expertise in multi-language sentiment analysis. Leveraging its cutting-edge AI, DMR offers context-specific insights across languages, affording startups invaluable local understanding.

Now, sentiment analysis operates on both structured and unstructured data. While structured data is organized and easily searchable (think databases), unstructured data is more chaotic, including texts, tweets, blogs, reviews, and more. AI-powered sentiment analysis tools like DMR's can tap into this vast sea of unstructured data, extracting meaningful insights that might otherwise remain obscured. These insights are a goldmine, revealing not just what consumers are saying, but how they feel about a brand, product, or trend.

But how does AI achieve this? Through deep learning—a subset of machine learning—that models its computations after the human brain with "neurons" or nodes. Deep learning algorithms process data with a complexity and depth that's reminiscent of human cognition. For sentiment analysis, these algorithms "learn" to understand context, semantics, and even sarcasm, ensuring that the extracted sentiments are not just accurate, but nuanced.

For startups, the implications can be profound. Harnessing these AI-driven insights enables them to navigate the market with an unparalleled level of agility. They can make data-driven decisions, refine their strategies in real-time, and anticipate market shifts—often long before competitors even get a whiff of change. In essence, platforms like DMR empower startups to be not just reactive, but proactive, seizing opportunities and addressing challenges long before they become mainstream.

In a dynamic market landscape, where change is the only constant, AI-driven social listening platforms are not just tools; they're essential allies, equipping startups with the insights and foresight to thrive and lead.

Market Research Resources

There is a huge array of market research resources ranging from customer research to syndicated services. Companies like Kantar, Ipsos, Gfk and Nielsen are the giants of the industry, but mostly relevant to those with large budgets. Then, there are the more specialized firms, especially for deep tech, such as:

- Forrester: A global research and advisory firm that provides reports on various markets, including effective GTM strategies.

- Gartner: Another global research firm that provides market research, consulting, and advisory services. Gartner is well-known for its Magic Quadrants, which evaluate vendors in a particular market and help businesses make informed decisions about which vendors to partner with.

- Frost & Sullivan: A global research and consulting firm that provides market research reports, industry analysis, competitive intelligence, and strategic advice.

- IDC: Another global research firm that provides market research, consulting, and advisory services. IDC focuses on the technology industry, but also has coverage in other areas such as healthcare, telecommunications, and manufacturing.

- ABI Research: A market research firm that focuses on technology and telecom. They provide reports, market data, and consulting services.

- Technavio: A market research firm that provides reports, market data, and consulting services. They focus on the technology industry.

In addition to these general market research resources, there are also a number of other resources available that deep tech companies can tap into. These resources can provide insights into specific technologies, industries, or markets. For example:

- Hello Tomorrow: A global non-profit organization that connects deep tech entrepreneurs with investors, mentors, and partners.

- Deep Tech Labs: A venture capital firm that invests in deep tech startups.

- Deep Tech Hub: A platform that connects deep tech startups with resources, partners, and investors.

The best market research resource for you will depend on your specific needs and budget. If you are just starting out, you may want to start with a general market research firm like Forrester or Gartner. Once you have a better understanding of your target market and your competitive landscape, you can then consider more specialized resources.

Of course, it is important to remember that market research is just one part of the business planning process. You should also conduct your own research, talk to potential customers, and get feedback from experts in your field. By combining market research with other forms of research, you can make more informed decisions about your business.

Product-Market Fit (PMF):

Achieving PMF is akin to finding the North Star for startups—it guides all subsequent endeavors. Traditional techniques to achieve PMF revolve around the iterative feedback cycle. Startups would introduce their product to a small segment of their target audience, gather feedback, refine the product, and reintroduce it. This cycle would continue until the product deeply resonated with the market's needs and desires.

Tools that have been fundamental in this journey include:

- **Surveys:** Tools like SurveyMonkey or Typeform allow startups to get direct feedback from users, often yielding detailed qualitative insights.

- **Usability Testing:** Platforms like UserTesting offer real-time feedback on product usability, providing insights on where users struggle and where they derive value.

- **Beta Testing Platforms:** Tools like BetaList or Product Hunt offer a platform for startups to introduce their offerings to an early audience, gathering real-time feedback and refining their product iteratively.

Enter the era of AI, and the landscape of achieving PMF has transformed. AI-driven tools, with their ability to analyze massive datasets, provide startups with quantifiable metrics on which product features resonate with users and which don't. For instance, platforms like Pendo or Mixpanel allow businesses to understand in-product user behaviors at scale, automatically identifying features that are hit or miss with users. Rather than waiting for weeks or months in the traditional feedback loop, startups can now pivot and iterate in mere days, accelerating the journey to PMF.

Customer Personas & Journey Mapping

Crafting customer personas and mapping their journey has been a cornerstone of effective marketing and product development. Traditionally, businesses would rely on focus groups, surveys, and interviews to understand their customers, creating static representations of their ideal user. Tools like Xtensio have made it easier to visualize and share these personas across teams.

However, in the digital age, when we can access huge amounts of user data, we have the capability to make these personas dynamic. AI-driven tools, such as HubSpot's CRM, not only help track customer behaviors but also predict future behaviors based on historical data. These dynamic personas evolve with real-time data, ensuring products and marketing campaigns remain in sync with shifting customer expectations.

IP Management

Intellectual property stands at the core of innovation. Traditionally, IP management was a tedious process, involving tracking global databases for potential conflicts and maintaining a vigilant eye on infringement. Tools and platforms, like Google Patents or the USPTO's Patent Search, have been very useful for basic tracking and search functionalities.

However, with the innovation landscape becoming more competitive, proactive IP management is crucial. Enter AI-driven IP solutions. Platforms like ClearView, integrated with AI, do more than just monitor; they anticipate. By analyzing global trends, patent applications, and IP registrations, these tools predict potential IP conflicts. For instance, if a startup in another country files a patent that closely mirrors yours, AI tools can provide real-time alerts, allowing you to modify designs or take preemptive legal steps. Subscription-based services like Innography or PatSnap offer detailed IP landscape insights, helping startups identify white spaces in the innovation landscape, potential collaborators, or even acquisition targets.

The fusion of AI with traditional tools and methodologies amplifies a startup's ability to innovate, protect, and pivot, fostering a resilient and forward-thinking approach in today's dynamic business ecosystem.

Strategic Analysis & Forecasting

Traditional tools like SWOT (Strengths, Weaknesses, Opportunities, Threats) and PESTEL (Political, Economic, Social, Technological, Environmental, Legal) have long been the bedrock of strategic analysis. These frameworks provide a holistic view of internal capabilities and external environmental factors. But in our rapidly changing world, there's a demand for forecasting tools that can predict future market dynamics.

Emerging AI-driven strategic tools like AlphaSense or Crux Informatics scrape vast amounts of data from the web, including news sources, financial reports, and more. They analyze economic indicators, political shifts, and technological innovations to forecast potential market disruptions and emergent opportunities. For instance, a startup in the renewable energy sector can get alerts on geopolitical events that might affect oil prices, allowing them to adjust strategies proactively.

Goal Setting and Dynamic Tracking

Goal setting has traditionally leaned on tools and methodologies like SMART (Specific, Measurable, Achievable, Relevant, Time-bound) and OKR (Objectives and Key Results). While SMART is centered around clearly defined and quantifiable goals, OKR pushes teams to set ambitious objectives and track progress through specific outcomes. Visual management platforms like Trello and Asana helped teams break down these goals into actionable tasks and track their completion in a collaborative environment.

But the agility of today's market requires more than static tracking. AI-enhanced platforms like BetterWorks or Lattice introduce dynamic goal management. For instance, if a startup is falling behind on its customer acquisition goals, these platforms might not only alert the team but might also suggest outreach strategies or even identify specific sectors or demographics where the traction is lacking.

Pricing Frameworks

Traditional pricing tools like Price Intelligently and Prisync rely on competitor price tracking and market benchmarks to suggest optimal pricing. By continuously scanning the market, they ensure that businesses remain competitive, and their pricing remains aligned with industry standards.

With AI's introduction, tools like BlackCurve or Pricefx have taken a giant leap. These tools can, for example, analyze consumer buying behavior during holiday seasons and suggest optimal discounts or offers to maximize sales while protecting profitability.

Sales and Marketing:

Historically, sales and marketing tools have centered on Customer Relationship Management (CRM) platforms like HubSpot and Zoho. These CRMs streamline tasks such as contact management, email marketing, lead scoring, and more. For instance, a sales representative can schedule follow-up emails, track lead interaction history, or even set up automated email campaigns based on specific triggers.

But the next evolution step lies in AI-powered CRM systems like Salesforce Einstein. Beyond automation, they introduce predictive analytics. Imagine a system suggesting the best time to reach out to a lead based on their interaction history or predicting which leads are most likely to convert into customers based on intricate behavioral patterns.

Performance Tracking and Analytics

Performance analytics has largely been dominated by platforms like Google Analytics, which allows businesses to track website visitors, source of traffic, on-site behavior, and much more. For instance, a startup could use Google

Analytics to see which marketing channels (like social media or pay-per-click advertising) are driving the most conversions, or which web pages have the highest bounce rate.

However, AI-enhanced platforms like Heap and Mixpanel push the envelope. For instance, if a specific blog post is generating high traffic, these platforms might analyze the type of content within the blog, the audience demographics, and even the user interaction to suggest similar content themes or strategies that can replicate or amplify this success.

Problem-Solving Through Scenario Simulations:

Before today's AI-driven models, startups used tools like MindTools or Gamestorming for brainstorming and problem-solving while developing scenarios and plans. But today, with platforms like AnyLogic or Simul8, AI can simulate complex business scenarios. Startups can play out entire campaigns, product launches, or even potential mergers in a risk-free virtual environment, tweaking strategies based on AI insights.

In this ever-evolving startup ecosystem, the fusion of traditional tools with AI isn't just beneficial—it's becoming essential. Startups that harness this synergy will inevitably find themselves better equipped to tackle upcoming challenges and gain competitive strength.

In essence, both your toolkit and strategies should be fluid, versatile, and responsive to the changing dynamics of your startup, market, and customer base.

APPENDIX D:
Product Launch Checklist

A successful product launch is essential for any company, but it can be especially challenging for academic startups that have no brand equity. As a result, they need to do a lot of upfront work to build awareness about their venture as well as the specific product.

The good news is that there are a number of things that academic startups can do to increase their chances of a successful product launch. We have already discussed the elements of a robust Go-to-Market strategy, what does into it and how to execute it. We also provided a relevant toolkit in Appendix A.

By following the checklist below, you can put yourself in a good position to launch your product and achieve your business goals.

Here is the checklist you can use:

Planning: This is a particularly critical stage of the product launch process. It is important to carefully plan every aspect of the launch, from defining your target audience to setting clear goals and timelines. A well-planned launch will help you achieve your desired results and avoid costly mistakes.

- Define your target audience: Who are you trying to reach with your product? What are their needs and pain points?

- Understand your customer needs: What are the features and benefits that your product will offer? How will it solve your customers' problems?

- Develop a unique value proposition: What makes your product different from the competition? Why should customers choose your product over others?

- Create a compelling marketing message: How will you communicate the value of your product to your target audience?

- Set clear launch goals: What do you want to achieve with your product launch? Do you want to generate awareness, generate leads, or drive sales?

- Develop a timeline and budget: When do you want to launch your product? How much money do you have to spend on marketing and promotion?

- Test and iterate your launch plan: Don't just launch your product and hope for the best. Test your launch plan with a small group of customers and make adjustments as needed.

Execution: This is the stage where you put your plan into action—you fail to execute well and the whole plan goes wasted. It is important to execute the launch in a disciplined and methodical way. This includes launching your product on time and within budget, promoting your product effectively, and collecting ongoing feedback from customers.

- Launch your product on time and within budget: This is essential for ensuring the success of your product launch.

- Promote your product through a variety of channels: Use diverse channels to reach your target audience, such as social media, email marketing, and paid advertising.

- Collect feedback from customers: Get feedback from customers early and often to make sure you are meeting their needs.

- Make necessary adjustments to your product or marketing strategy: Based on the feedback you receive from customers, make necessary adjustments to your product or marketing strategy.

Monitoring: This is the final stage of the product launch process and it is also vital as it is your way of ascertaining what is working and what is not. Most importantly, you will know when to pivot if needed. Do this based on evidence, not gut feeling.

- Track your launch metrics: Track your launch metrics, such as website traffic, social media engagement, and sales, to measure the success of your launch.

- Analyze your results: Analyze your results to identify what worked well and what could be improved for future launches.

- Make improvements to your launch process: Based on your analysis of your results, make improvements to your launch process for future launches.

APPENDIX E:
Incubators Vs Accelerators

The main difference between an incubator and an accelerator for academic startups is the stage of the startup that they are designed to support.

Incubators are typically geared towards early-stage startups, often those that are still in the ideation or prototyping phase. They provide startups with a supportive environment to develop their ideas, access to resources such as office space, equipment, and mentorship, and help them to connect with potential customers and investors. Incubators may also offer training and workshops on a variety of topics, such as business planning, marketing, and fundraising.

Accelerators are designed for startups that are further along in their development, typically those that have a working prototype or MVP (minimum viable product) and are ready to scale their business. Accelerators provide startups with intensive mentorship and support, access to a network of investors and advisors, and help them to prepare for fundraising and growth.

Accelerators typically last for a fixed period of time, such as three or six months, and often culminate in a demo day where startups pitch their businesses to potential investors.

Here is a table that summarizes the key differences between incubators and accelerators:

Characteristic	Incubator	Accelerator
Stage of startup	Early-stage	Growth-stage
Duration	Typically 1-5 years	Typically 3-6 months
Focus	Developing ideas and prototypes	Scaling business
Funding	May provide funding, but typically does not take an equity stake in startups	Often provides seed funding in exchange for an equity stake in startups
Mentorship	Provides mentorship and support, but may be less intensive than an accelerator	Provides intensive mentorship and support
Network	May provide access to a network of investors and advisors, but may be less extensive than an accelerator	Provides access to a network of investors and advisors

Which is right for you?

The best way to decide whether an incubator or an accelerator is right for your academic startup is to consider your specific needs and goals. If you are still in the early stages of development and need help to develop your idea and prototype, an incubator may be a good fit for you. If you are further along in your development and are ready to scale your business, an accelerator may be a better option.

It is also important to note that some incubators and accelerators offer programs specifically for academic startups. These programs can be a great way to connect with other academic entrepreneurs and get the support you need to succeed.